Praise for
Case Studies in Disability-Driven Innovation

Author Robert Ludke makes it abundantly clear that companies engaging the unique perspectives of people with disabilities are likely to foster resourceful, adaptive, and ultimately profitable cultures. This is a book for all businesspeople.

—Cary Griffin, Author,
Making Self-Employment Work for People with Disabilities

"Bob Ludke's *Case Studies in Disability-Driven Innovation* is a must-read for investors like me who see the transformative potential of an inclusive economy. This book doesn't just spotlight the untapped market opportunities in the disability sector—it proves that disability-driven innovation is a blueprint for sustainable growth, market expansion, and unparalleled social impact. As someone who champions ventures at the intersection of profit and purpose, I can confidently say: Bob's insights are essential for those ready to lead the future of business."

—Chris Maher, Founder and CEO, Samaritan Partners

"If you are committed to a more accessible and inclusive future, this book needs to be on your list!"

—James Warnken, digital accessibility specialist,
entrepreneur, and consultant

"This book encapsulates innovative strategies and practical techniques to work towards a more inclusive community for individuals of all abilities."

—Amanda Myers, Employment Coordinator,
Down Syndrome Innovations

"Disability and entrepreneurship are two sides of the same coin—both demand resilience, innovation, and the skill to navigate a world not built to fit you. *Case Studies in Disability-Driven Innovation* highlights the untapped power of disabled entrepreneurs. Imagine if we recognized Disability as a competitive advantage from the start—how many more game-changing innovations could we unlock?"

—Diego Mariscal Founder,
CEO & Chief Disabled Officer of 2Gether-International.

"People with disabilities remain the largest population of Americans underrepresented in our workforce and economy. *Case Studies in Disability-Driven Innovation* is the 2025 roadmap for all employers, from Main Street to Wall Street, to transform the way we harness disabled talent in our workplaces and expand our base of new U.S. taxpayers."

—Sara Hart Weir, Executive Director,
Kansas Council on Developmental Disabilities

"In a sea of voices that hear only limitations when it comes to entrepreneurs with disabilities, Bob's work is the soundtrack we've been waiting for to celebrate the innovation that's inherently driven by entrepreneurs with disabilities. He illustrates a compelling narrative of the vitality of entrepreneurs with disabilities as secret weapons of growth, value creation, and out of the box problem solving for every organization."

—Ashton Rosin, Head of Investor Relations, FirstMark Capital

"If there's one thing I want readers to take away from this book, it's this: disability-driven innovation benefits us all. It's not just about creating a more inclusive world. It's about unlocking a treasure trove of creativity and ingenuity that can make our lives better."

—Joseph Jones, Chief of Staff,
President's Office, Des Moines University

Praise for
Transformative Markets

Published in 2020, the premise of Robert Ludke's *Transformative Markets* is that, if society is to thrive in the future, the markets we use every day must become powerhouses for driving innovative and sustainable goods and services.

"From the moment you pick up this book, it will pull you in. It's a rare combination of a critical message and truly actionable information about markets that is written compellingly. It's a book that is full of great stories and data adding up to a clear and hopeful path forward."

—Elizabeth Sturcken, Managing Director,
Environmental Defense Fund

"Bob is the first author to demonstrate how we can spur the development of sustainable markets so they are a force for advancing global social progress. *Transformative Markets* is a must-read if you have a spirit for innovation, a desire to make a real difference in people's lives, and a passion for improving the planet."

—Michael Green, Chief Executive Officer,
Social Progress Imperative

"Sustainability is more than getting better relative to yourself. In this ambitious book, Bob Ludke explains what sustainability really means, the distinctions between sustainable and unsustainable markets, and the role of all of us in transforming markets to support a truly sustainable future. The book is full of clear examples and recommendations to help translate the ideas into tangible action that can (and need to) begin right now."

—Cory Searcy, Professor, Ryerson University

"With a clear, compelling case for using market forces to drive sustainable business practices, *Transformative Markets* is a must-read. This book offers fresh ideas for addressing the most critical issues of social and environmental responsibility."

—Susan Kahn, Managing Partner, 44 Degrees North Partners

"No long-term challenge is more pressing for global business leaders than building sustainability into their business models. But you can't achieve that goal without first understanding how societies can build markets that meet our needs in the present without compromising our future. In his new book *Transformative Markets*, Ludke makes enormous progress in defining what sustainable markets are, and what they are not. *Transformative Markets* should be on every CEO's reading list."

—Andrew Sullivan, Partner, Hudson Pacific

"This is a beautiful book. *Transformative Markets* gives vision and clarity on how we must transform our ways of producing and consuming so that we create a better future for the next generation."

—Michele Sofisti, Board Member, Global Conservation Corps

Case Studies in Disability-Driven Innovation

Robert Ludke

Case Studies in Disability-Driven Innovation

ISBN: 979-8-89576-057-4 (Paperback)
ISBN: 979-8-89576-058-1 (Hardback)

Published by:

Contents

Dedication and Acknowledgements..9

Introduction:
Why We All Need More Disability-Driven Innovation 13

Chapter 1:
A Roadmap for a More Inclusive, Innovative Future.........................31

Chapter 2:
The Curb Cut Effect: The Secret Sauce of Transformative Change.. 54

Chapter 3:
Understanding and Appreciating Disability 64

Chapter 4:
The Disability Employment and Innovation Landscape 84

Chapter 5:
The Human Toll of Employment Disparities 105

Chapter 6:
The Disruptions to Employment and Innovation.............................127

Chapter 7:
Innovating to Transform 161

Chapter 8:
Creating Markets for Disability-Driven Innovation..........................186

Chapter 9:
Surpassing the Tipping Point..208

Notes 226

Dedication and Acknowledgements

Case Studies in Disability-Driven Innovation is dedicated to all those dreamers, doers, and entrepreneurs on the cutting edge of innovating a better future – no matter the challenges. The promise of a better tomorrow is possible because of you.

If there's one thing I want readers to take away from *Case Studies in Disability-Driven Innovation*, it's this: disability-driven innovation benefits us all. It's not just about creating a more inclusive world; it's about unlocking a treasure trove of creativity and ingenuity that improves our lives.

Each of us has a stake in fostering more disability-driven innovation across the globe. It's not just the responsibility of policymakers, advocacy organizations, or big corporations; it's also something each of us can – and must – contribute to.

How? By supporting those incredible innovators and entrepreneurs who are changing the world. Invest in their businesses, connect them with your networks, introduce them to potential customers, or simply buy their products. Every action, big or small, can help fuel this movement and create a brighter future for everyone.

The best part of writing a book is it is an opportunity to meet new people, reconnect with old friends, and create a network of amazing collaborators. My life is richer and more fulfilled because of the people that joined me on this journey.

To that end, I would like to acknowledge all those who made *Case Studies in Disability-Driven Innovation* possible. Your insights added greatly to my learning and made for a much more insightful and compelling book.

- Jarrett Alley, Ballpark Services Manager, Kansas City Royals
- Jack Anderson, Disability Advocate, Down Syndrome Innovations
- Archer Archer, Public Policy Consultant, Archer's Public Policy
- Allison Aslan, Disability Program Analyst, Office of Global Programs, U.S. Department of State
- Hannah Bouline, Director of Impact and Sustainability, Vertical Harvest
- Victor Calise, Director Global, Belonging, Accessibility Center of Excellence, Walmart
- Erica Cole, Founder and CEO, NoLimbits
- Keely Cat-Wells, Co-Founder, Making Space
- Caroline Croft Estay, Co-Founder and Chief Potential Officer, Vertical Harvest
- Marianne Dijkshoorn, Founder, Welkom Accessibility & Events
- Giorgi Dzneladze, Founder, Georgian Wheelchair Workshop
- Michael Fembek, CEO, Zero Project
- Tami Fenner, Business Coach and Advisor
- Steve Foresti, Senior Advisor, Wilshire Associates
- Jenn Guinty, Coordinator, Events and Guest Services, Kansas City Royals
- Austin Hanson, Austin Hanson, Paralympic athlete and Member, Kansas Council on Developmental Disabilities
- Sara Hart Weir, Executive Director, Kansas Council on Developmental Disabilities
- Chanda Hermanson, Administrator of Disability Employment and Transition Division, Montana DPHHS
- Jolene Iyer, Global Sustainability and ESG Lead, Adobe

- Joseph Jones, Chief of Staff, President's Office, Des Moines University
- Michael Hess, Founder and Executive Director, Blind Institute of Technology
- Emilea (Em) Hillman, Owner, Em's Coffee Co.
- Andy Imparato, Executive Director, Disability Rights California
- Eric Ingram, Space industry expert and founder of Space Scout
- Cara Elizabeth Yar Khan, CEO, The Purple Practice
- Regina Kline, Founder & Managing Partner, Enable Ventures and Founder, SmartJob
- Sandy Lacey, Executive Director, Howe Innovation Center & Perkins Solutions
- Ashlea Lantz, Co-Founder, Value Inclusion, LLC
- Carly Listman, Corporate Communications and Public Affairs, Adobe
- Amanda MacFarlane, Assistant to the CEO, Vertical Harvest
- Chris Maher, Founder and CEO, Samaritan Partners
- Diego Mariscal, Founder, CEO, and Chief Disabled Officer, 2Gether-International
- Sarah Mark, Director of the Workforce Navigators program, Salesforce
- Kayla McKeon, Director of Grassroots Advocacy, National Down Syndrome Society
- Mason Metzger, Founder of Universal Design Works
- Amanda Myers, Employment Coordinator, Down Syndrome Innovations
- Hannah Olson, CEO, Disclo
- Caitlin Pettit, Director of Event Services, Kansas City Chiefs
- Joe Quintanilla, Vice President of Development and Major Gifts, National Braille Press

- Ashton Rosin, Head of Investor Relations, FirstMark Capitall
- Michelle Sagan, Director of Communications and Marketing, National Down Syndrome Society
- Sean Stone, Facilities Lead, Vertical Harvest
- Nino Tabidze, Project Coordinator at Coalition for Independent Living
- Genevieve Thompson, Manager of Advocacy, National Down Syndrome Society
- Nikki Thompson, Grow Well Associate, Vertical Harvest
- Katherine Toops, Co-Founder, JT Firestarters
- Ana Tsitsagi, Project Coordinator at Coalition for Independent Living
- James Warnken, digital accessibility specialist, entrepreneur, and consultant
- Robin Tim Weis, Director of International Affairs, Zero Project
- Michael Zalle, Founder and CEO, YellowBird

INTRODUCTION

Why We All Need More Disability-Driven Innovation

When money, rather than innovation or value,
is your competitive advantage, that's when
things get boring and stagnant ...
—Hank Green, the chief executive of Complexity, an educational
media company, who identifies as having a learning disability that
interferes with sensory processing

"I just want to make sure that when I start at Austin High School in August, the school will be accessible for me," said Archer Archer in May 2011 to the staff and faculty of Austin High School, located in Austin, Texas (USA). He was reassured that Austin High School would most certainly be ready for his arrival on campus in a few months.

On the first day of school, Archer arrived at a campus that most certainly was not accessible to a student like him using a wheelchair. The automatic doors he'd been promised had not been installed. There was only one elevator. Walkways from one part of campus to another were uncovered and open to the elements.

The following year, in May 2012, Archer met with school officials to request accessibility features be added to the Austin High School Campus. Again, he was assured that the improvements would be made before he returned to school for the start of his sophomore year.

In May 2013, Archer again met with school officials to request that accessibility features be added to the Austin High School Campus. Again, he was assured that the improvements would be made before he returned to school for the start of his junior year.

In May 2014, Archer met with school officials once more to request that accessibility features be added to the Austin High School campus. Again, he was assured that the improvements would be made before he returned to school for the start of his senior year.

One morning in September 2014, Archer arrived at the Austin High School campus in a driving rainstorm. The accessible doors he'd asked for over three years ago had still not been installed. As had been the case every day for the past four years, he had to wait for someone to open the doors – rain or shine. Archer's patience had long since worn thin – and he was now soaking wet. And cold.

Next, he waited for the elevator to take him to the second floor, where he again had to go outside in the pouring rain. The covered walkway he'd asked for four years before had still not been built. Now, even more wet and cold, he again had to wait for someone to open a door for him – another door lacking an automatic opening function.

When he finally reached his classroom, Archer decided he'd had enough. If the school was not going to improve, he would force it to improve. Maybe he wouldn't benefit from the improvements – he was a graduating senior – but students after him would.

Archer called his mom and told her he was done with being patient. Then he prayed. He was told simply and unequivocally in his prayers, "Go."

And go he did.

Archer got bids to install three automatic door openers at Austin High School – the cost: $40,000.

Like all seniors, Archer had to complete a Capstone project to graduate. His project was to raise money to install the three automatic door openers. Along the way, Archer planned to educate his fellow students, teachers, and school staff on the importance of accessible educational institutions.

When Archer told his Capstone teacher of his plan, he was met with skepticism. The most any student had raised in a Capstone project was $3,000.

Archer soon launched the Mr. Maroo Challenge (named after his school's mascot). Modeled after the wildly successful ALS Ice Bucket Challenge, designed to raise awareness of amyotrophic lateral sclerosis (ALS), the Mr. Maroo Challenge would challenge students to spend an entire day in a manual wheelchair. Students could either pay $20 to challenge another student, faculty, or school staff to use a wheelchair, or the challenged person could pay $20 to decline the challenge.

Due to Archer's popularity in school and the challenge's importance, it quickly became a hit among the Austin High School community. The problem, as Archer quickly realized, was that $20 here and $20 there would not get him to his $40,000 goal.

A couple of weeks into the challenge, Archer wrote an open letter to the Austin community outlining his purpose and objective. The letter struck a chord across Austin. Instead of collecting $20 at a time, Archer started receiving checks for $50, $100, and even more. One of his neighbors contributed $25,000.

Then, the business community joined in. Major Austin employers like H.E.B. and Alamo Drafthouse supported the campaign, as did internationally known brands like Amazon and Nike.

Within a month, the Mr. Maroo Challenge had raised nearly $90,000. Not only were three automatic doors finally installed on the Austin High School Campus, but 32 automatic doors were also installed in the seven other high schools in the Austin Independent School District. Each of the schools benefited from hosting its version of the challenge. Hundreds of students, faculty members, and staff gained a first-hand appreciation of how inaccessible much of our society is for people without full mobility.

The impact of the Mr. Maroo Challenge and the various challenges that came from it went beyond Austin, Texas. The Mr. Maroo Challenge grew into Archer's Challenge, touching thousands of people and raising over $1 million. Even better, Alamo Drafthouse soon installed automatic doors at many of its theaters across the US, all of which have wheelchair-accessible seating.[1]

The (Harsh) Reality of Entrepreneurship and Innovation

A former investment banker and serial entrepreneur, Rachel Greenberg, wrote it best, "Entrepreneurship isn't about making something you – the founder – want or like. It's about making something your audience wants or needs and doing so as scalably, effectively, and cost-efficiently as possible."[2]

Many times in this book, we will read about entrepreneurs who did not start a business because they were passionate about their product or service. Instead, like any good founder, they studied the market and created a company that matched their strengths and market opportunity.

Although *Case Studies in Disability-Driven Innovation* profiles many exciting ideas and impactful outcomes, there is no doubt that innovation is hard and there is zero guarantee of success. You can have a rich parent, be backed by a star-studded venture capital firm, or work in the research and development department of a Fortune 500 company bankrolling your idea. Unless your idea meets your audience's needs – and does so in a manner that is better than the competition's idea - it will fail.

Going Back to School the Next Day

Michael Zalle was born with two congenital abnormalities – first, his hand. Doctors theorized in the 1970s that he'd suffered the rare circumstance of embryonic rings around his right wrist area, which, therefore, did not develop. The outcome was a "little hand" caused by restricted blood flow. The second, and much more severe surprise, was that Michael had been born with a neural tube opening that was not fully closed. This spina bifida occurs during pregnancy, resulting in incomplete spinal development. Michael's case was fortunate as his body "filled the hole" with tissue but he was still left with a lifetime of neurological complications due to the tethered spinal cord not "releasing" during early growth/development years.

Today, Michael is the founder and CEO of YellowBird, a $35 million company located in Arizona with over 20 employees. Michael describes YellowBird as "a professional gig platform that quickly and easily connects vetted and certified environmental, health, safety, and risk professionals to opportunities on-demand. YellowBird uses matching technology to connect the right people, in the right location, with the right experience for the job."

The most time-consuming and stressful part of Michael's job is the constant demand to raise financial capital so YellowBird can continue expanding. Like most technology companies, venture capital is the most viable way to raise the needed funding. Yet, that is never easy.

"I'll be candid. One of our venture capitalists is my only impact investor. He wants perfection," said Zalle. "If we don't have the right people doing the right things at this time, or I'm not doing as well as I can, he is all over me. He makes these demands on the business. I often respond, 'I would love to do some of those things, but I'm underfunded right now.' Or I'll say, 'Look, we're going to get there. But I do not have the funding right now to hire that person.' And he's like, 'Well, you gotta cut somewhere else because you gotta get this.'"

Zalle continues, "You have to remember if you're a tech startup, you're running out of money every single day until you're profitable. I'm not going to be profitable till next year. The venture guys care only about the return on investment for their money. It is up to me to figure out how to make that happen. While the investors may appreciate my backstory about my disability, they are going to treat me like any other entrepreneur. Which is fine with me."

Then Zalle made the connection between living his whole life with a disability and growing the resilience to overcome the challenges he faces every day at YellowBird.

"Honestly, I've had my spirit broken many times through this journey, even with YellowBird. That has nothing to do with my disability. I get kicked in the teeth all the time. You literally have payroll on Monday, and your investors tell you on Friday, 'I'm sorry we aren't putting any more money in.' I then have to go to my wife and say, 'We gotta pull money out of our IRA because I need to pay these people.' Again, that is a reality of being a founder and a CEO. It has nothing to do with disability. But it has a lot to do with courage. If there is one word to describe being an entrepreneur, it's courage. You must have courage to be an entrepreneur and an innovator. You just get up every single day and do the best you can do with your abilities."

"That's why not everybody can do this. You are going to have scary moments. It doesn't matter if you are a straight, white male or a female with a disability. I remember that conversation with my wife about the payroll as clear as day. I had to pull $200,000 out of my IRA. I'm 49 years old. I will need that money soon. Even worse, that $200,000 came without a guarantee that YellowBird would get more money anytime soon. That day, I could not see a path to more funding. If YellowBird implodes, I'll need to get another job. I have a family. I need an income."

"So, you've got all of that going through your head, and your emotions, and your heart. And it is the scariest frigging thing that anybody can ever go through. It really is. It's that gut check moment that will tell you if you are actually an entrepreneur."

"Honestly, it's like showing up for school the next day. Like when I was on the playground and the whole class takes their arm and starts mimicking an amputated arm on the playground. The ringleaders got everybody to do this. The whole class was walking up to Mikey when he's five to make fun of his disability. It was humiliating but I had to get up the next day and go back to school. That's what it's like being an entrepreneur."

Defining Innovation

Let's begin this journey by understanding innovation – a topic we will discuss in greater detail in Chapter 7. A good starting point is a definition of innovation. A January 2008 article in *Stanford Social Innovation Review* by James Phills and his colleagues at Stanford University defines innovation as: "... a process or outcome must meet two criteria. The first is novelty: Although innovations need not necessarily be original, they must be new to the user, context, or application. The second criterion is improvement. To be considered an innovation, a process or outcome must be either more effective or more efficient than preexisting alternatives."[3]

Perhaps more importantly, Phills and his colleagues make it clear that the magnitude or scale of the innovation or its impact is not part of its definition. They rightly note that such judgments are highly subjective. What matters is the improvement that resulted from the innovation.[4]

With this explanation in mind, yes, some innovations have a broader reach and impact than others. However, that does not diminish the fact that any innovation that allows for an improvement compared to existing alternatives is, in fact, innovation.

Appreciating the nature of the "newness" in the innovation is essential. "An innovation is an idea, practice, or object that is perceived to be new by an individual or other unit of adoption," wrote Everett Rogers in *Diffusion of Innovations*. "It matters little, so far as human behavior is concerned, whether an idea is 'objectively' new as measured by lapse of time since its first use or discovery. The perceived newness of the idea for the individual determines his or her reaction to it. If the idea seems new to an individual, it is an innovation."[5]

In this context, Archer's use of technology to automatically open doors at his school was not a discovery or innovation of technology. Automatic door openers were first brought to market in the 1950s. Rather, Archer's innovation came from a new use of an established technology by an individual who needed to solve a challenge that was impacting his life.

Rogers also introduces an important concept of time in his definition. For an idea to become an innovation, it must spread through a market and gain acceptance promptly.[6] Otherwise, the adoption rate is so slow the innovation never takes hold. As a result, the "newness" fades, and someone else may (or may not) pick up on the idea. Again, go back to Archer's challenge. The idea of the challenge needed to quickly gain the interest and support of Archer's fellow students and the Austin community. If Archer could not get people to join the challenge, there was no potential for innovation. Another student at a different school at some point in the future would be credited with the idea of launching a challenge to make their school more accessible.

Defining Disability-Driven Innovation

Disability-driven innovation has no precise definition. Jeetah Roubeena of the Mauritius Research and Innovation Council put forth a narrow definition: "... the creation of novel products, processes, technologies, or services or the promotion of novel ways of thinking for implemented solutions that have implications, especially for people with disabilities and their entourage."[7]

While there is nothing inherently wrong with that definition, it is too narrow as it confines disability-driven innovation to solutions specific only to persons with disabilities or their close associates. Disability-driven innovation is much broader, much more impactful, and benefits all of us every day – regardless of whether we identify as disabled or have a close connection to disability.

A better definition of disability-driven innovation is, "A disability-centric process grounded in the principles of inclusive design that proactively generates new and novel ideas, products, or services that solve a human need, especially for persons with disabilities. It can occur within an organization – intrapreneurial – or outside an organization – entrepreneurial. The innovation may ultimately have a broader market appeal and benefit end users of all kinds. Yet, the initial intent of the innovation starts with meeting an immediate need within the population of people who identify as disabled."

Faster Capital, an online incubator and accelerator based in Dubai, provides a helpful overview of inclusive design – a concept at the heart of disability-driven innovation:

"Inclusive design goes beyond mere accessibility; it aims to create products, services, and environments that cater to the diverse needs of all individuals, regardless of their abilities."

Here are some inclusive design concepts outlined by Faster Capital to consider:

- Holistic Approach: Inclusive design considers the entire user experience, from conception to implementation. It involves collaboration among designers, engineers, and end-users to ensure that no one is left behind.

- User-Centered Design: Inclusive design starts by understanding the unique challenges faced by people with disabilities. By actively involving them in the design process, we gain valuable insights that lead to more effective solutions.

- Universal Design Principles: These principles guide inclusive design. For instance:

  o Equitable use: Products should be usable by everyone, regardless of their abilities.
  o Flexibility in use: Designs should accommodate a wide range of preferences and abilities.
  o Simple and intuitive: Complexity should not hinder usability.
  o Perceptible information: Information should be conveyed effectively through various senses.[8]

Like Phill's definition of innovation, disability-driven innovation does not mention scale or impact. However, it does open the door to improvement, whether for an individual or the global marketplace of consumers.

Case Studies in Disability-Driven Innovation will demonstrate that innovation takes many forms. Innovation is not just about bringing the next cool gadget or the latest smartphone version to market. It is not about trying to be the next "unicorn" that secures millions of dollars in venture capital funding. Instead, innovation is about bringing together different lived experiences and diverse ways of tackling problems to find solutions that address a human need. *Case Studies in Disability-Driven Innovation* will focus exclusively on innovation led by persons with disabilities or through their active participation. This book will showcase them as active participants rather than passive recipients of innovation led by non-disabled persons.

Just a few examples of disability-driven innovation that we encounter in everyday life include audiobooks, automatic doors to make public spaces more accessible, a consulting business to help companies apply universal design principles so their offices accommodate all employees, and children's toys that accurately reflect our different life experiences. The pace of disability-driven innovation is accelerating. As mathematician and best-selling author Hannah Fry discussed in her Bloomberg podcast series, innovations ranging from robot avatars to bionic limbs are quickly revolutionizing how persons with disabilities participate in the workforce.[9]

Keely Cat-Wells – an entrepreneur, disability rights advocate, and co-founder of technology and media company Making Space – raises a point about the value proposition of disability-driven innovation we must never forget or dismiss. More important than the economic value it generates or the gadgets it creates, disability-driven innovation involves creating a more equitable society. It is about us as people. As Cat-Wells reminds us, "We often speak about the business case of disability and the amount of money that companies are leaving on the table without including us. Disability innovation leads to this opportunity to not have to legitimize our existence based on the economic power that we hold but rather to focus on human rights and civil rights while driving change."[10]

Disability-Driven Innovation in Their Own Words

To set the stage for the rest of the book, consider the words from entrepreneurs and innovators about the mindset of disability-driven innovation. Many of these words and their stories underscore just how hard it is to be an innovator with a disability. Yet, they all persevere because they want to create value for people and enrich lives. None stop innovating. And all of them make the world a little better.

It stems from solving problems specific to the community. Most of the entrepreneurs I meet have a very personal connection to the problems they are solving. They have lived experience with disability. That means they start with an inclusive design approach which by default creates more accessibility for more people. And I think that's pretty special about people who are living and working within the disability community. What they are building is not only good for people with disabilities, but the broader population as well.

—Chris Maher,
Founder and General Partner, Samaritan Partners

Disability-driven innovation really thinks about and recognizes inclusion. Yes, it fosters creativity, but it also unlocks opportunity, and it helps businesses think about the future needs of their buyers and their consumers. This ultimately helps build their business and create a better trajectory for their business as a whole.

—Hannah Olson, CEO, Disclo

The value proposition of disability-driven innovation is that it emphasizes making products, environments, experiences, and opportunities accessible for everyone, regardless of their ability level. On the surface, it may appear as though my work in disability-driven innovation only benefits people with disabilities. However, I find that going beyond the requirements established by the Americans with Disabilities Act to create experiences, environments, and products that are accessible to everyone, allows my clients to understand their existing customers' needs better, tap into new target markets, and serve communities to the fullest extent possible.

—Mason Metzger, motivational speaker,
consultant, and founder of Universal Design Works

It's ideas and practical solutions that a person with a disability comes up with and then leverages them to drive change in particular areas they're involved in.

—Victor Calise, Director Global,
Belonging, Accessibility Center of Excellence, Walmart

Growing up with progressive vision loss, my vision has gotten worse over the last 17 years. I have to be okay and comfortable with change ... knowing that what works today might not work tomorrow, and what worked yesterday doesn't work today. Being okay with that is the first step to the innovation process. It's a mixture of self-motivation and self-discipline where you can't just settle. You can't go with the flow and ride the wave. You have to go against that grain and say, "That's not right. That's not okay. What can I do about that?"

—James Warnken, digital accessibility specialist,
entrepreneur, and consultant

The Use of Case Studies in This Book

Many skeptics, including Greg Satell, a well-known business advisor and expert in how ideas spread among people, question using case studies as a research method. Compared to other forms of qualitative or quantitative research, case studies are believed to be methodologically weak because they often rely on very small sample sizes and overly focus on positive outcomes.

Another valid criticism is that case studies tend to be "within a case" rather than "across a case." A paper by Malin Knutsen Glette of the University of Stavanger (Norway) and Siri Wiig of the Western Norway University of Applied Sciences provides a helpful distinction between the two concepts. "Within-case analysis describes the details of each case and its themes" by deeply exploring a subject but not going beyond that specific subject. In contrast, "Cross-case analysis identifies differences and similarities across cases and investigates the findings' applicability to similar settings."[11] Thus, an over-reliance on case studies tends to miss broader trends and learnings because the focus is on within-case analysis rather than cross-case analysis.

However, *Case Studies in Disability-Driven Innovation* will overcome the methodological weaknesses of a case study-based approach through the following:

- Combining insights from case studies with those of desktop research and interviews with subject matter experts

- Using case studies to demonstrate the practical implications of other forms of research used in the book

- Seeking those involved in the work featured in the case studies to be as open about the challenges and barriers as they are about the ultimate successes

- Drawing insights and analysis of a broad cross-section of case studies examining many forms of disability-driven innovation, thus employing a cross-case analysis

A SWOT Analysis of Disability-Driven Innovation

Another method by which this book will overcome the methodological concerns of case studies is to make an honest assessment of where disability-driven innovation is today, and where it could be going in the future.

Without a doubt, the case studies in this book are about successful innovations. While much can be learned from loss and failure, the objective of sharing these case studies is that each provides lessons allowing disability-driven innovation to scale into something beyond immediate innovation.

Below is a SWOT analysis of the current state of disability-driven innovation. SWOT analyses allow people to gain a comprehensive and unbiased assessment of the strengths, weaknesses, opportunities, and threats facing a concept like this. Please note the acronym "PWD" is used for the sake of brevity in the SWOT analysis when referring to persons with disabilities. This book otherwise attempts to avoid referring to persons with disabilities by an acronym, unless it is directly quoting someone else or their research.

Later chapters of the book contain a more detailed analysis of disability-driven innovation; the analysis below is a good starting point for our expedition into the exciting worlds of entrepreneurship, innovation, and transformation.

Image 1: SWOT Analysis of Disability Innovation (DI)

Strengths	Weaknesses
• Because disability is diverse, its impact is widespread as DI creates value for investors, companies, communities, and society • The goods and services created through DI allow for greater accessibility for all through a more universally-designed world • DI is a pathway to entrepreneurship and meaningful careers for millions of PWD	• DI has yet to consistently scale to create a truly inclusive and accessible society for all • The ability and opportunity to innovate and scale ideas is inconsistent, and there is not a clear pathway to structurally improve DI • PWD face many structural barriers that prevent DI from reaching its full potential
Opportunities	**Threats**
• DI can permanently transform society to one that is inclusive and equitable for all • DI (and the associated manufacturing and delivery of services) can drive sustained socio-economic growth across the world • The demand for disability-assistive products and services is enormous – and growing with the global PWD population projected to reach 3.5 billion by 2050	• Structural barriers – poor public policy, discrimination, lack of investment – could permanently derail DI from its full potential • Innovators in DI are more at risk of ideas being coopted than non-disabled innovators • If DI does not reach its full potential, millions of PWD are consigned to a life of lower socio-economic opportunity

Image description: A four-quadrant grid outlining the strengths, weaknesses, opportunities, and threats facing disability-driven innovation.

Always Remember the Core Market for Disability-Driven Innovation

Case Studies in Disability-Driven Innovation is filled with excitement and optimism about the transformative potential of disability-driven innovation to reach global markets worth trillions of dollars. Yet, Erica Cole and her company No-Limbits is a powerful reminder that, at its core, disability-driven is about making the world more accessible and inclusive for persons with disabilities. The definition of disability-driven innovation used in this book is a "disability-centric process grounded in the principles of inclusive design that is proactively generating new and novel ideas, products, or services that solve a human need, especially for persons with disabilities."

In 2018, Erica was involved in a car accident that caused her left leg to be injured so severely it had to be amputated. The multiple corrective surgeries on her leg forced Erica to give up a promising career in chemistry with a job offer at Los Alamos National Laboratory waiting for her.

"In the beginning, No Limbits was just my way of using the skills that I had. I was a costume designer in my free time. I actually put myself through college making costumes for people for things like Renaissance Fairs and Comic Cons," recalls Erica.

She continues, "I made this transition from being a chemist to launching an alteration shop for folks with disabilities, mainly amputees, because those were the folks that I was interacting with. I then realized that there was not a market for adaptative clothing. Tommy Hilfiger was making some adaptive clothes but no one else was. So, I put a pitch together to launch an adaptive clothing company and I was accepted into the Target Corporation's Accelerator Program. Once I was done with that program, I launched a Kickstarter campaign to raise money for the company. When that was going on, the producers at Shark Tank saw my pitch and invited me to be on the show. I received a $1 million investment from Mark Cuban from my Shark Tank pitch."

With initial funding secured, No Limbits furthered its product line. Its clothing ranges from pants and jeans with specially designed zippers to quickly access prosthetic devices to sensory-friendly shirts for people with autism and ADHD, adaptive wheelchair pants, and leggings and jackets for those with limited dexterity.

After two years of spectacular growth, an unexpected and seemingly unrelated development happened – in 2020, Apple released its iOS 14 update. Sometimes referred to as ATT (App Tracking Transparency), the iOS 14 update allows users to disable the tracking features of apps used on various mobile devices. While protecting consumer privacy is very important, the update seriously affected No Limbits. Erica continues,

"It seems like a minute detail, but the iOS 14 update really hurt – for a lot of reasons. Before the update, we were able to specifically target amputees and other persons with mobility limitations for our ads. We had people with a wide variety of disabilities coming to our website looking for solutions to their challenges. So, we decided to expand our product assortment to all kinds of disabilities. But now with the update we can't target our core demographic. We can't even target our ads to Paralympians. Even worse, there are all these people with disabilities who no longer know our products exist – products that can help them."

"We have had to change how we reach customers. We do a lot more in-person marketing. We advertise our products as healthcare products, try to engage with veterans, and even rely on referrals within healthcare organizations. But there is no way to efficiently reach the disability market after iOS 14. That is a huge roadblock for us and for making clothing and fashion more accessible for consumers. There are a lot of consumers with disabilities who do not even know that adaptive clothing products exist."

No Limbits designs and produces adaptive clothing specifically for people with mobility limitations—people living and working with disabilities. Adaptive clothing is different from universal clothing, which everyone can use regardless of disability. The seemingly well-intentioned motivation behind the iOS 14 update—protecting personal privacy—has created a significant barrier to creating a market of disability-driven innovation explicitly intended for the core market: people with disabilities.

Erica's story is one to remember always. We must continually strive for innovation to be accessible first to the community most in need. Once that objective is achieved, it is a wonderful development when the innovation finds its way to the mass markets, creating lasting value for all.

CHAPTER 1

A Roadmap for a More Inclusive, Innovative Future

Companies that operate on their past may not have a future.
—No attribution but a proven fact

Since the fall of the Berlin Wall in 1989, Blockbuster, Kodak, Borders, Pets.com, PanAm, and even the iconic General Motors have either gone bankrupt, been bought, or just ceased to exist. Every one of them stopped innovating and did not meet changing market expectations. A key reason? They failed to attract the next generation of talent that could push them to improve, create a new line of products to satisfy consumer demand or invent ways to create long-term value.

Despite the unprecedented rise in earnings and share value generated by most Fortune 500 companies in recent years, it is a given many of them will suffer the same fate in the coming years. They, too, will be consigned to the dustbin of history – ancient relics quickly forgotten or, at best, laughed at as the punchline of jokes.

There is a way forward. It requires an entirely new approach to maximizing human talent. We must no longer focus on what people *cannot* do. Instead, we must use all our many different abilities so that our diverse lived experiences drive innovation.

Case Studies in Disability-Driven Innovation will serve as an actionable resource for leaders and executives across the global economy to foster competitive, integrated employment for persons with disabilities. Competitive, integrated employment for disabled persons is not charity or philanthropy. Instead, it is a management strategy that encourages innovation and long-term value creation for companies, investors, consumers, and society. It is a powerful antidote for what ailed once well-known brands like Compaq and Tower Records – companies that were once dominant players in their respective markets but failed to adapt to changes in consumer needs. Neither exists today.

The entrepreneurs and organizations profiled in this book will demonstrate that competitive, integrated employment allows companies of all kinds to seize market opportunity, enjoy higher and sustainable profits, and better innovate to maintain market leadership. The reason is simple – living with a disability necessitates innovation. As Haben Girma, a human rights lawyer and the first Deafblind graduate of Harvard Law School, wrote, "Disability creates a constraint, and embracing constraints spurs inventive solutions. Our history has numerous examples of people with disabilities leading advances in science, technology, and other fields."[12]

Eric Ingram, a space industry expert and founder of Space Scout – a space observation service provider focused on space domain awareness – made a powerful connection between disability-driven innovation and meaningful market opportunity. As he said in an interview, "I talk all the time with would-be entrepreneurs with disabilities. Almost all of them are interested in creating a business or innovating something to help people with disabilities. While I appreciate that desire I always ask, 'What is the market for that?' I always tell them it is much better to build something that is accessible to everyone. That market is huge. Often the most simplistic solution benefits everyone. A niche solution only applies to a niche market."[13]

Case Study: Em Hillman – Leaving a Sheltered Workshop to Innovate a Better Community

At birth, doctors told her mom that Emilia (Em) Hillman would never walk, talk, or feed herself due to a condition called agenesis of the corpus callosum – the absence of nerve tissue connecting the right and left sides of her brain.

Despite their predictions, Hillman graduated from high school, where she had the opportunity to gain work experience starting her freshman year. Gaining entry-level work experience as a young teenager strengthened her expectations and desire to work.

After high school, Hillman started working in a sheltered workshop – the only option available in her small town of Independence, Iowa (U.S.) – where she earned well below the minimum wage for two years. To put it mildly, Hillman was very unhappy in the workshop. She was underpaid, stuck in a job she did not want, and no thought was given to helping her create a life-long career.[14]

The workshop also could have been a better fit for who Hillman is as a person. It didn't allow her to interact with customers, be social, and use her natural ability to sell. She was prevented from interacting with customers and separated from her non-disabled colleagues. Instead, Hillman and her disabled colleagues were consigned to working in a back room of the facility. Hillman was not in a role at the workshop that highlighted her at her best. Instead, it was a role assigned to Hillman based on her disability and a presumption of others' low expectations.

In February 2009, Hillman left the workshop. In December 2009, after months of planning and preparation, she opened Em's Coffee Co.

Hillman did not start Em's Coffee Co. because she is passionate about coffee (in fact, she does not drink coffee). Instead, owning and operating a coffee shop fits Em's personality and skill set. She likes being around people, the business provides a sense of community for her and others, and, most of all, she loves being "the boss." However, Em's Coffee Co. is more than just a job that allows her to be the boss. She is the sole owner of the business. She has what every entrepreneur wants – the responsibility and freedom to ensure their venture endures and prospers.

Beyond the direct benefits to Hillman, her coffee shop has become a critical piece of the social infrastructure of a small community in a rural part of the United States. Through her desire to be around people, Hillman has innovated a welcoming space for an entire community where people can find companionship.

As has been written about Em's Coffee Co., "The beauty of Em's Coffee Co. is that it works for her and her community. Em's tagline personifies the shop and all that has gone into creating it: 'It's way more than a great cup of coffee.'"[15]

The schedule at Em's Coffee Co. proves that point. "As soon as we open on Wednesdays, we have all the men from the Lutheran church," said Tami Fenner (Em's mother). "Then, at nine o'clock, all the women from the Lutheran church come here. On Fridays, we have a group of Christian women who meet, and then there is a men's coffee group. We also have another elderly men's coffee group that comes here on Mondays, Wednesdays, and Fridays. And we have just gotten busier and busier every year. We have customers who visit us even though they live hundreds of miles away."

Despite the enduring success of Em's Coffee Co., Em Hillman and her family repeatedly stress that owning a coffee shop (or any small business, for that matter) is not for everyone and is not the employment solution for every aspiring entrepreneur. Much work has gone into building Em's Coffee Co., and it continues every day. Hillman arrives at 6:15 a.m. each morning, and the doors open at 6:30 a.m. sharp. Hillman, her mother, and the job coaches oversee a team of six employees, two of whom identify as disabled.

Hillman and her family also strive to ensure the coffee shop provides an excellent experience for everyone. "When we first started the coffee shop, I didn't want it to be a second-class type place," stated Tami Fenner. "One of the things I've always said is that if you start with secondhand stuff, they will always treat Em like a second-class citizen. So, we researched and researched and researched everything about the business. Em went to a barista school. She also took a course on how to serve gelato. She has a great cup of coffee. In fact, we have one lady who comes a lot. She always says, 'I drink coffee all over the world, and this is the best coffee I've ever had.'"[16]

While this book will praise the success stories of disability-driven innovation, we must remember that the constraints necessitating innovation for persons with disabilities are often dehumanizing and barriers to being more included in society. There is the reality of desperation behind many of these innovations. Em Hillman does not love coffee. Her coffee shop represents an innovation that makes her life more fulfilling. Hillman's alternative was working in a sheltered workshop at a sub-minimum wage. To her credit, Hillman's innovation improved her life while also enriching the lives of the people in her community of Independence, Iowa.

The Factors Behind Disability-Driven Innovation

Various factors spur disability-driven innovation. It is often "bottom-up" – people innovating to improve life in an unaccommodating society. Much bottom-up innovation is not created by altruistic motives to improve the world or sell a startup to a venture capital firm for millions of dollars. Instead, many entrepreneurs who identify as disabled are simply trying to improve their lives and have no other recourse but to create homegrown solutions.

Ashton Rosin, Head of Investor Relations, FirstMark Capital, an early-stage venture capital firm, made an essential distinction between the motivations of founders with disabilities and those who are not disabled. One is motivated by the challenge of solving a problem. The other is motivated by an opportunity to capitalize on a situation. Rosin said:

> *Over the last 10 years, we have had this glamorous ecosystem where lots of capital is flowing in. TV shows were being made about these crazy big companies that were being created through venture capital. And then lots of people started showing up and wanting to build companies and be startup founders. Most of them were unsuccessful. But then you start to parse out the profiles inside of those failures. Very few of those kinds of founders wanted to build these companies because they needed to. That is different than entrepreneurs with disabilities. I see them building companies because they need that innovation. Or they have an idea to be catalyzed because it needs to exist in a world not built for them. The others see an exciting problem. They think there could be a lucrative solution. Or the government just passed some big law where there's a lot of subsidy money. So, they think. "Let me go build that thing." Their motivation is starting from a very different place.*

Consider the business model of Wazi, an eyewear brand based in Uganda. Wazi is revolutionizing the eyecare industry by offering high-quality, fashionable eyewear designed by African artisans. Launched in 2017 by Ugandan entrepreneurs Brenda Katwesigye and Georgette Ndabukiye, Wazi's mission is not to dislodge Oakley or Ray-Ban from the market. Instead, Wazi aims to reduce the stigma around eyecare health and improve access to eye testing and treatment – and do so in a region of the world where such care is not always available.

Other times, innovation occurs "top-down," often in an established enterprise motivated to bring new products or services to market that can benefit the company. A pharmaceutical company bringing a new drug to market to treat depression or Alzheimer's is an example of a "top-down" innovation.

We use disability-driven innovation without even thinking about it. Any parent pushing a young child in a stroller or traveler with a roller bag suitcase has taken advantage of sidewalk curb cuts. This disability-driven innovation meets the needs of countless people every day.

Acknowledging that disability-driven innovation is not perfect or foolproof is also essential. Seemingly great ideas have fallen flat, countless entrepreneurs could not turn their ideas into reality, and others could not gain sufficient market share. There also have been many products brought to market that seemed like a great idea at the time but were quickly met with derision when brought to market – the stair climbing wheelchair and the sign language glove are two prominent examples.

Turning an innovative idea into a viable business or achieving competitive, integrated employment in a professional setting is hard work, no matter if the employment occurs in a one-person business or a large corporation. It is a journey of months, years, and even decades. Every organization and person profiled in *Case Studies in Disability-Driven Innovation* experienced setbacks and moments of profound doubt and discomfort in their journey. Yet, they persevered thanks to a powerful combination of grit, collaboration, an appreciation of the benefits of diversity, and a commitment to a better, more inclusive society. Lives are enriched, consumers enjoy products and services meaningfully impacting their lives, trillions of profits have been earned, local and global markets accessed, and investors are rewarded through higher shareholder returns.

I hope that *Case Studies in Disability-Driven Innovation* inspires the next generation of business leaders to invest in the innovative potential of persons with disabilities, be they solo entrepreneurs or part of a larger organization. Regina Kline, a disability rights lawyer and early-stage investor in disability-focused start-ups, remarked, "If we talk about mere participation in the labor force, we get locked in, we get pushed into a corner. We need to be talking about leading – not just participating. There is absolute evidence that in the last 50 to 100 years, people with disabilities have been at the front of the line in developing innovative products. They just have not been recognized or renumerated for it."[17]

We must also focus beyond the current workforce and our present ways of innovating. Suppose society expects a steady stream of innovations and increases in productivity. In that case, ensuring the pipeline of talent coming into the workforce is diverse and inclusive of all abilities is essential. Reaching the so-called "opportunity youth" between ages 16 and 24 is more important than ever. Yet significant gaps exist when it comes to providing training, mentoring, and internship opportunities to populations that often face barriers to employment – such as persons with disabilities.

Maximizing every employee's innovative potential will generate competitive, integrated employment globally. Doing so requires genuine, authentic leadership. None of this is easy. Yet the payoff is enormous. No matter if it is measured by the progress in human potential or the growth of the global economy.

We must appreciate the uniqueness of this moment. A consistent theme in conversations about this book is that the mindset of disability and its value proposition is changing. Ashlea Lantz, a co-founder of Value Inclusion, a boutique consultancy founded on the belief that disability inclusion creates lasting value, said it best: "We are now part of this cultural evolution that sees disability-driven innovation as profit. There is a huge mindset shift underway. Namely, to go from disability as a deficit to disability as a profit. I don't mean to profit off disability. Rather, realizing that disability equals creativity, and it often results in innovation. Disability-driven innovation is the innovation that is designed for the whole spectrum of society. It starts with the outliers, which then, in turn, makes things universal for all people. The profit comes when more and more people can use something and benefit from it."[18]

Going from Innovation to Transformation

It was suggested that this book be titled *Case Studies in Disability-Driven Transformation*. The argument is that disability-driven innovation is transformational. While that argument makes a lot of sense, I decided to stick with the original title of *Case Studies in Disability-Driven Innovation*. The reason is that innovation by persons with disabilities (or for persons with disabilities) has yet to fundamentally transform the lives of people who are disabled, our economy, or society more broadly. Yes, many disability-driven innovations have markedly improved the lives of millions – perhaps even billions – of people. However, those innovations have not had a catalytic effect on the global economy. Nor have they created an inclusive, accessible society for all.

This is not to blame entrepreneurs or business owners with disabilities, nor is it to blame innovators creating solutions to make society more inclusive and accessible. As the book will demonstrate, amazing people and powerful companies are doing incredible things to innovate a better world. Instead, we must accept that our mindset about how the economy functions is what prevents disability-driven innovation from scaling.

The good news is – and we will cover this in Chapter 9 – I believe we are tantalizingly close to reaching the "tipping point" where disability-driven innovation has a transformative impact across society and the global economy. But, again, we are not yet at that point.

The Biggest Impediment to Achieving Disability-Driven Transformation

Myth: Money is the biggest impediment to bringing more disability-driven innovation to our economy.

Reality: The biggest impediment is our economy's siloed way of innovating.

Our inability to understand the big picture and coordinate accordingly prevents disability-driven innovation from becoming a disability-driven transformation. In speaking with entrepreneurs, researching this book, and exploring how markets grow and scale, it is clear that the biggest impediment to transforming society through disability-driven innovation is what Mats Larsson, a consultant and technologist, terms "development silos."

Understandably, an innovator is highly focused on bringing their idea to market, be it an assistive technology device, a new software, or a restaurant. However, the downside is that "Each specialist area is like a silo" in which "researchers, engineers, experts, and employees who work in each of their respective silos are more likely to promote their areas of development" rather than "to take the time and money needed to map the landscape of development silos."[19]

Research by the Howe Innovation Center at Perkins School for the Blind found that development silos also occur in the field of disability innovation – to the detriment of persons with disabilities who need the products resulting from the innovation. In the Howe Innovation Center's 2023 report entitled, *Defining DisabilityTech: The Rise of Inclusive*

Innovation, four challenges were identified in creating products and services for the market of people with disabilities:

1. Companies focused on people with disabilities often serve a dispersed user community. It can be challenging for innovators to connect to the right user base and maintain an engaged user pool for continuous product feedback.

2. Assistive devices serve smaller markets with price-sensitive customers, making it difficult to achieve attractive economics. This is especially true for hardware products. As a result, people with disabilities often pay a "disability tax" for products that serve only the disability community.

3. Both private and public sector stakeholders serve key roles as gatekeepers to solutions, often determining which technologies are available to a community, even if better-matched products exist in the market (e.g., regional distributors, employers, federal government quotas, state agencies).

4. The typical challenges for entrepreneurs – product design, funding, market entry, hiring, partnership – become more daunting for founders of Disability Tech companies which are initially targeting a smaller group of users with unique requirements.[20]

In that regard, innovation in disability-centric markets is no different than any other innovation in the global economy. Innovators are – rightfully so – focused on their ideas. However, just because an idea will create a lot of value for many people does not mean it happens. Barriers and silos of all kinds exist in every market for every product or service. And if an innovation does happen, sometimes it is cost-prohibitive given the nature of the market it serves.

Reinforcing the perverse nature of the development silos is the fundamental tenant of a free-market economy and shareholder capitalism. Virtually every major company in the world – and countless smaller ones – is governed by the belief that its primary goal is to maximize profits. The best idea doesn't always win. All too often, the idea that can generate the most immediate profit wins. Rather than stepping back to think about the most significant value and the long-term, leaders worldwide are conditioned to plunge ahead and maximize the amount of money over the shortest period. "We live in a shareholder economy now. Investors push companies to focus on the short term. Quarterly financial results, not long-term lasting impact – social and financial considerations. Get your money in and out as quickly as you can with maximum financial return," ruefully noted Chris Maher, founder and general partner of Samaritan Partners, a public benefit venture capital fund focused on early-stage companies in the disability sector.[21]

The challenge – and the imperative – is for the rest of us to help innovators by better understanding the landscape in which innovation materializes and where collaboration opportunities exist to scale that innovation. We must give innovators, investors, executives, and policymakers the courage to think and act long-term with a mindset that seeks to achieve the greatest value for all. Hopefully, this book meaningfully advances that effort.

Committing to Disability-Driven Innovation

An organization's commitment to disability-driven innovation exceeds the business's four walls. While any organization must seek to maximize the value proposition of disability-driven innovation to ensure that its house is in order by creating an inclusive and accessible environment, a genuine commitment extends to the communities where the company operates and throughout its entire supply chain. It must act in a way that creates an innovation ecosystem rather than holding its work.

A company that commits to disability inclusion across its entire value chain can be considered a "disability-inclusive business." The team of disability experts at the United Nations Economic and Social Commission for Asia and the Pacific developed a helpful definition for a disability-inclusive business: "Disability-inclusive businesses are maximizing opportunities across their value chains by ensuring that the primary functions of business (sourcing, operations, logistics, product design, marketing, and sales and services) benefit from the application of a disability-inclusive lens across the business value chain and the inclusion of persons with disabilities as leaders, employees, customers and suppliers/ distributors."[22]

As this topic is explored in greater detail throughout *Case Studies in Disability-Driven Innovation,* it becomes clear that authentic leadership on inclusion, product design, human resources policies, workplace accessibility, and purchasing decisions has a ripple effect throughout global supply chains. Best practices in creating disability-inclusive businesses serve as a model others can – and will – emulate.

Values Versus Value

The many ways we innovate goods and services raise an essential distinction between "values" and "value." Values are our personal collection of beliefs that often culminate in our "moral compass" – the framework by which we differentiate right from good, good from evil, and just from unjust. Everyone reading this book has a personal value set that appreciates the importance of fostering a more inclusive society. Businesses also have distinct values – often called "purpose" – that try to combine market strategy and social good. For example, Coca-Cola endeavors to "Refresh the world. Make a difference." Starbucks asserts, "As it has been from the beginning, our purpose goes far beyond profit. We believe in the pursuit of doing good."

However, disability inclusion is not about imposing one's values on others or a company showcasing a statement of purpose to customers. Disability inclusion drives innovation that creates value – original goods and services that can meet human needs while responsibly generating profits over the long term. As noted, much of disability-driven innovation is about a person with a disability trying to create value in their life – sense of purpose, income, becoming more integrated into society, and so on.

While it is impossible to quantify that aspect of disability-driven innovation, the business case for the value-creating potential of disability inclusion is compelling. Consider:

- The Center for Talent Innovation determined that 75 percent of employees with disabilities in the United States have ideas that would drive value for their company compared with 61 percent of employees without disabilities.[23]

- Research by faculty at London Business School discovered that 74 percent of human resources professionals surveyed noted that their teams had begun to work better together since incorporating persons with disabilities into their organizations.

- The same research found that 75 percent of human resources professionals indicated that hiring employees with disabilities enhanced the general atmosphere in their organization.[24]

Equally compelling is the market opportunity and business performance that comes from disability-driven innovation.

Consider:

- According to Return on Disability, a Toronto, Canada-based consultancy, the global PWD population is roughly 1.58 billion people – more than the estimated 1.4 billion people who live in

China. Further, "With a conservative estimate of each PWD having 1.85 friends or close family members, the disability market directly touches an additional 2.9 billion individuals globally – 41 percent of the global population."[25]

- The global assistive technology market is projected to exceed $31 trillion by 2030. Assistive technology is defined as items or equipment that help "people with impairments increase, enhance, or retain their functional abilities."[26] Eyewear, hearing aids, canes, and scooters are examples of assistive technologies.

- Research by Accenture shows that companies inclusive of people with disabilities are, on average, twice as likely to have higher total shareholder returns than their peers, 28 percent higher revenue, and 30 percent higher profit margins.[27]

In its "Global Economics of Disability Report: 2024," Return on Disability makes a powerful observation about how value is created – for individuals and across the economy:

The most important rule for capturing value in disability is that experience drives shareholder returns, not compliance. This is true for both consumers and employees. PWDs do not demand accessibility. PWDs do not demand the minimum standard, that a product or experience be minimally usable. They demand consistent, positive experience, relative to context – what we call "delight." As an employee, this can mean the trade-offs of upward mobility, compensation, work-life balance, and colleague relationships. As a consumer, this can mean ease of purchase, useability, and those "wow" factors that create brand ambassadors. This is true across the customer journey, from the initial shop to the completion of the experience.[28]

The value creation mindset applies to entrepreneurs and corporations alike. It involves finding an opportunity in the market that can be filled with a new product or service. It means creating a workforce built on competitive, integrated employment. The motivating factor often is the shared desire to thrive and be prosperous – something each of us can appreciate.

Case Study: Walmart: Creating a More Accessible and Inclusive Shopping Experience – and Driving Business Value

Walmart - the world's largest retailer by sales - is sustained by an exceptionally strong and values-based culture. For Walmart, culture isn't a "feel good" exercise or marketing slogan. Rather, it is a competitive differentiator in the marketplace.

In 2018, Walmart CEO Doug McMillon wrote,

> *Right now, we're focused on dialing up our inclusiveness. The right and smart thing for Walmart is to... cultivate inclusive environments in every part of our business - every store, every club, every distribution center and every part of our Home Office locations all over the world. Our people make the difference, and we need every one of them performing at their very best...Leading in an inclusive way is foundational to living out our value of Respect for the Individual.[29]*

In 2023, Walmart took an unprecedented step to create a more inclusive shopping experience for all its customers – and doing so in a way that embodies its commitment to Respect for the Individual. Starting in the late summer of 2023, from 8 a.m. to 10 a.m., Walmart began a sensory-friendly hours pilot project at all of its nearly 5,000 stores in the U.S. During those two hours each day, the stores were transformed into a more serene and calming shopping experience. All in-store TV walls were changed to a static image, the store radio was turned off, and the lights were lowered wherever possible.

Because so many shopping environments can be intense for people sensitive to bright and flashing lights, large crowds, or loud noises, they often resort to online shopping – which could further their sense of isolation.

Particularly for those with ADHD, dyslexia, or PTSD, Walmart's "sensory friendly hours" offered a welcoming, inclusive shopping experience. As one parent wrote to Walmart, "As a mother of a child with autism, thank you very much for recognizing needs, and being sensitive to them. Little things such as lighting, noise, etc. does make a difference."[30]

The sensory-friendly hours have also made a difference for store associates. Victor Calise, Director Global, Belonging, Accessibility Center of Excellence at Walmart, remarked, "We have received positive feedback from associates who are benefitting from the quieter work environment and feel like Walmart did this for them, too."

The feedback from the three-month pilot project was overwhelmingly positive – from Walmart's customers to its store associates. Creating a sensory-friendly experience transformed the shopping experience and the workplace environment for hundreds of thousands of employees. In November 2023, Walmart announced it was indefinitely continuing sensory-friendly hours in all U.S. stores.

It took work to achieve sensory-friendly store hours every day in every store. As with every large, profit-driven organization, Walmart's accessibility team had to demonstrate that the sensory-friendly hours helped the business. Extensive internal communications were needed both leading up to the start of the pilot phase and the long-term expansion. Walmart also listened to feedback from its store managers and associates because, after all, they operate the stores.

The potent ingredient in these internal discussions was Walmart's cultural commitment to respecting the individual. As Calise noted, "It was because of Walmart's culture that we could drive this idea. The customer is always number one. I mean, that's respect for the individual. You wouldn't work at Walmart if you didn't believe that, right? And so, as a cultural moment or opportunity or way to act on the culture, people said, 'Okay, I need to now pay attention to this. I need to make this work.'"[31]

Walmart has experienced strong business results and positive customer feedback in the U.S. since launching sensory-friendly hours. The company has now expanded the hours to its international markets with more than 3,000 locations in Mexico and more than 400 stores in Canada. This global amplification has been met with enthusiasm from both Walmart customers and associates.

Walmart is not stopping at sensory-friendly hours. In 2024, Walmart introduced Caroline's Carts in its stores. Caroline's Carts are designed for caregivers supporting many people, including those with disabilities, children, seniors, and people with limited mobility or injuries. Walmart plans to equip all Supercenters with two Caroline's Carts and all Neighborhood Markets with at least one, totaling about 12,000 carts nationwide. Walmart expects every store to have its allotment of carts by early 2025.[32]

Finally, in 2024, Walmart launched a partnership with Aira. This app connects people who are blind or have low vision to professional visual interpreters for secure access to visual information anytime, anywhere. It began by piloting Aira's on-demand visual interpreting service at all Walmart locations in California, Texas, and Florida at no cost to customers. Beginning in December 2024, Aira is now offered in all U.S. stories. The Aira service is available 24/7/365 through the Aira app. Aira's professional visual interpreters can enhance a user's experience at Walmart by describing products, looking for sales, checking out, and helping with in-store pickup.[33]

Walmart's benefits are wide-ranging and far-reaching. The Aira App allows customers to have more accessible and easy shopping experiences – which is also good for business. Customers of all kinds are taking advantage of the sensory-friendly hours – not just those who identify as disabled. Customers with cataracts, those recovering from an illness, or those who want a more serene shopping experience regularly visit the stores. Caroline's Carts can be used by a caregiver of a person with a disability or a parent bringing kids to the store.

The Exciting Future of Disability-Driven Innovation

We must acknowledge that disability-driven innovation has shortcomings and that only some products have worked as intended. We must also see that it is not the panacea for every problem facing the global population of people with disabilities. By itself, disability-driven innovation will not achieve competitive, integrated employment, solve pay disparities in the workplace, make housing more accessible, or generate better health outcomes for disabled persons. Nor will it solve existential threats to society, such as poverty or climate change.

However, as *Case Studies in Disability-Driven Innovation* will demonstrate, a disability-inclusive mindset has proven time and time again to drive innovation that provides lasting value to society – investors, employees, consumers, entrepreneurs, and communities alike. Persons with disabilities are, by their very nature, innovative. We spend every day innovating around a world not made to accommodate disabilities. Our very existence depends on innovation.

The benefits from disability-driven innovation impact every individual, community, and organization on the planet. Appreciate the innovation taking place outside the formal structure of the economy. Understand that much of that innovation is driven by an urgency to achieve personal and professional self-worth. Imagine the influx of new ideas at a company where twenty to thirty percent of its workforce feels empowered to bring their best, most authentic selves to work daily. Then, consider the value to be created if all those employees were permitted to rechannel the ingenuity of masking disability instead of applying creativity, resourcefulness, and resilience to their jobs.

The most exciting aspect of disability-driven innovation is that it is now part of a global movement and will become more prevalent soon. As Robin Tim Weis, Director of International Affairs at Zero Project, a global and research-driven initiative to support the implementation of the Convention on the Rights of Persons with Disabilities (CRPD), remarked:

> *In 10 years, the concept of disability-driven innovation is likely to be perceived as an integral part of mainstream innovation, celebrated for its contributions to societal progress and economic growth. This shift will be driven by several key factors, first and foremost the global demographic trends that will lead to aging populations in all continents – which leads to a growth in the number of people who acquire disabilities. The evolving concept of disability must be viewed through an intersectional lens that will highlight the diverse experiences and contributions of persons with disabilities, integrating their perspectives into broader innovation processes. Moreover, older disabled populations will exert stronger political pressure on government from a vantage point of disability confidence and not disability charity. Overall, disability-driven innovation will be treated not just as a niche area but as a crucial driver of broader societal and economic advancements.[34]*

Case Study: Mattel's Barbie with Down Syndrome – A Partnership to Adapt to a Diversifying Market

Mattel's Barbie doll is the best-selling toy in history. Launched in 1959, Barbie is sold in over 150 countries and enjoys 99 percent brand awareness. Barbie has over 19 million followers across social media platforms. The Barbie YouTube channel has over twenty million global subscribers and 23 billion minutes of content watched, making Barbie the number one girls' brand on YouTube. Not to be outdone, The *Barbie* movie became a cultural phenomenon in 2023 as it shattered multiple box office records and grossed more than $1.4 billion in box office sales.[35]

Despite more than six decades of success, Barbie has had her share of ups and downs. Most poignant, in 2011, Mattel began to realize that Barbie was falling out of fashion in its market. From 2011 to 2015, Barbie lost 30 percent of its market share to competitors, mainly because she no longer reflected the diversity in its customer base.

With declining market share, Mattel conducted in-depth research to understand how customers felt about the famous doll and determine whether more inclusive Barbies presented a substantial market opportunity. The results were startling. Richard Dickson, COO and President of Mattel Inc. said, "Moms increasingly viewed the brand as vapid, one-dimensional, and worse, literally uninspiring." [36]

The irony is that the doll was "conceived as a toy to inspire girls to think differently about their futures."[37]

The findings led to an expansion in the diversity of the dolls and Mattel's overarching customer strategy. In 2016, "the company expanded the So in Style line of Black dolls to include more skin tones, eye colors, and hair types, and also introduced Barbies with a range of body types."[38]

As Mattel diversified Barbie, the Down syndrome community became more vocal in wanting representation in the product line. Combined with the market power of the disability community, the chorus of voices led Mattel to embark upon creating the first-ever Barbie with Down syndrome.

When Mattel decided to move ahead with Barbie with Down syndrome, one of the first calls it made was to the National Down Syndrome Society (NDSS), seeking input in the design and marketing of the doll. "Mattel reached out to us for our expertise. Another reason was they wanted to be authentic in creating the doll. It was important for Mattel to create this doll in a partnership, and they wanted to show consumers true partnership and collaboration in making the doll," said Michelle Sagan, Director of Communications and Marketing at NDSS and an early participant in the engagement.[39]

NDSS convened a large group of experts, including its leadership and marketing teams, the health team, and one of its medical doctors on the NDSS Clinical Advisory Board. More importantly, two NDSS employees with Down syndrome – Kayla McKeon (Manager of Grassroots Advocacy) and Charlotte Woodward (Education Programs Associate) – were fully integrated into the collaboration with Mattel.

The process started with refining sketches of the doll to gather all the nuances of Down syndrome in terms of physical appearance, including considerations like the size of the eyes and ears, the crease in the palm, and the shape of the face. The design involved many tradeoffs. Subtle features of the doll were discussed, like adding a scar near the heart because many individuals with Down syndrome undergo heart surgeries. Yet only some things could be included in producing one doll model.

Mattel and NDSS operated with a spirit of openness and honesty throughout the process. There was much give and take from both sides.

All involved knew that, ultimately, the design had to gain the approval of McKeon and Woodward before it went into production.

Once production commenced, Mattel and NDSS collaborated on the doll's packaging and marketing. Both organizations "took full ownership of the doll," asserted Sagan. "We had to get it right for our community."

Barbie with Down syndrome has been a great hit from a market standpoint. The doll quickly sold out, and sales have been so strong that Mattel has already released a second version of the doll – a Black Barbie with Down syndrome.

More important than the market success is what the dolls represent. As Kayla McKeon said, "When I was a young girl with Down syndrome, I never thought there would be dolls with Down syndrome. But now seeing a doll with Down syndrome makes a world of difference."[40] Perhaps even more impactful is the opportunity for kids from all backgrounds to play with diverse toys. "Everyone should be playing with a Barbie with Down syndrome because kids and adults need to see the world differently," declared McKeon. "We are all diverse and the Barbie dolls that we play with should represent that."[41]

CHAPTER 2

The Curb Cut Effect: The Secret Sauce of Transformative Change

Technology is nothing. What's important is that you have faith in people, that they're basically good and smart, and if you give them tools, they'll do wonderful things with them.

—Steve Jobs, an American businessman, inventor, and investor best known for co-founding Apple who identified as dyslexic

The so-called "curb-cut effect" is a great way to understand the transformative value proposition of disability-driven innovation. Angela Glover Blackwell, the Founder in Residence at PolicyLink, coined this concept in a 2017 *Stanford Social Innovation Review* article.

Curb cuts were implemented in the United States after World War II to make sidewalks and streets more accessible for disabled veterans. The first documented implementation of a curb cut was in 1945 in Kalamazoo, Michigan.[42] Unfortunately, not much happened on the spread of curb cuts until the early 1970s. In Berkeley, California, disability rights activists Ed Roberts, Hale Zukas, Steve Brown, and the group of students known as the "Rolling Quads" began pressing the City of Berkeley to "build curb cuts on every street corner in Berkeley." Their call to action sparked the world's first widespread curb cuts program. Rumor has it that Roberts and the team also sped up the adoption process of curb cuts by pouring cement on street corners to make impromptu curb cuts.[43]

Blackwell powerfully conveys the enduring value that curb cuts created for all of us: "Then a magnificent and unexpected thing happened. When the wall of exclusion came down, everybody benefited – not only people in wheelchairs. Parents pushing strollers headed straight for curb cuts. So did workers pushing heavy carts, business travelers wheeling luggage, even runners and skateboarders."[44]

By 1980, the curb-cut movement spread to Denver, Colorado, when "disabled people in Denver staged a protest demanding curb cuts. They'd already blocked traffic until city transit officials promised to put wheelchair lifts on all the buses. Demonstrators in wheelchairs leaned over, for the photographers, to whack at concrete curbs with sledgehammers."[45]

Just over a decade later, the Americans with Disabilities Act was enacted. That landmark legislation "requires curb ramps and ramps to be installed along any accessible route in a public area, along a path where there's a change in height greater than ½ inch."[46]

Today, curb cuts are not just a fixture in U.S. cities – they are used worldwide in communities of all sizes.

When a society excludes people from participation and denies access to some, everyone feels the consequences. A sense of community is lost. People can't find jobs. Employers can't find workers. Creativity and innovation are stifled. Economic growth is impeded.

Conversely, Blackwell's curb-cut effect makes a case for the ripple effect of disability-driven innovation. "The curb-cut effect illustrates the outsize benefits that accrue to everyone from policies and investments designed to achieve equity. The country must choose: Will we make these investments? Will we make sure that everyone has access to the essentials for living productive lives – things like jobs and reliable transportation? Or will we neglect entire communities and waste the talents and potential of tens of millions of people?"[47]

Case Study: Making Creativity Accessible Through Artificial Intelligence

Steve Gleason is a former player for the New Orleans Saints of the National Football League. In 2011, he was diagnosed with ALS and has dedicated his life to telling his story and raising awareness of the incurable disease. Art has been a passion of Steve's for most of his life. Even with the loss of functionality in his arms and hands because of ALS, Steve has not stopped creating. Through a partnership with Adobe, Steve is not only able to make art, but he can also show it for the New Orleans community to appreciate.

Starting with sketches Steve created before his ALS diagnosis, he uses Adobe Firefly – an artificial intelligence-powered platform that can generate images and apply artistic styles by using text descriptions – to create beautiful art. Steve combines Firefly with custom eye-tracking technology that turns his eye movements into text prompts, which in turn, tells Firefly what to create. Adobe and Steve hope this collaboration is a starting point for unleashing a "global wave of creativity" for all people.[48]

Image 2: Artwork by Steve Gleason

No tree can grow to heaven unless its roots reach down to hell.

Image Description: Artwork created by Steve Gleason depicting a tree with its roots reaching under the ground. Image created by Steve Gleason and printed with permission of Steve Gleason.

The Curb-Cut Effect in All of Us

You do not need to be an innovator, investor, or entrepreneur to advance the curb-cut effect in your community or circle of friends and family. All of us can play a role in curb-cut transformations, be it through how we spend money, interact with others, or use our connections with others to promote an idea or innovation created by a person with a disability.

Nor is the curb-cut effect limited to "outside the box" ideas, disruptors, protestors, or early-stage innovators working on the economy's fringes. So-called legacy companies – established brands that have been in business for an extended period – must constantly be at the forefront of innovation and growing their market reach. If not, they'll lose their relevance and eventually go bankrupt or be bought by competitors. Disability-driven innovation must be essential to a legacy company's market and growth strategy.

Consider Disney Shanghai. In 2016, the Walt Disney Company opened its Disney Shanghai theme park, which was designed from the start to incorporate various accessibility features, such as attractions that are accessible to wheelchair users, displays in Braille, and sign language interpretation for certain shows.[49] Yes, Disney had to follow legal requirements that had been established by the Shanghai municipality and the People's Republic of China that mandated certain accessibility features. However, the park managers also wanted it accessible to as many people as possible. Their logic is simple – the more people who pay to enter the park, the better it is for Disney's bottom line. Excluding people from spending money on your product is a terrible business idea.

While rare, disability-driven innovation can have such a significant cross-over effect into mainstream markets that consumers with disabilities feel excluded from the market. A recent example is Nike's 2021 launch of its Go FlyEase shoe. Designed to be easy to take on and off, the Go FlyEase was "designed for disabled people, meant to solve a need for a market that hasn't historically had cool footwear options from big brands." The problem was that the shoe's launch was so successful that it immediately attracted a swarm of global buyers. As market supply quickly dwindled, the only place the Go FlyEase could be found was on the online platforms of secondary market sellers – with the shoe's cost more than double its original $120 price point. The supply chain constraints in 2021 prevented Nike from quickly bringing more shoes to the market. As a result, a seemingly accessible shoe for the disabled market suddenly became inaccessible.[50]

Those drawbacks notwithstanding, the Go FlyEase idea again proved that products designed to be accessible to all have a powerful influence on markets, and large numbers of consumers will actively seek to purchase them.

How Change Works

Greg Satell is a prominent author, academic, and C-suite business advisor who has spent much of his career exploring how ideas spread across networks of people and communities (be they physical or online). Satell has found that change does not occur in a "top-down" or "bottom-up" manner. Instead, change occurs "side-to-side."[51]

"Change never happens all at once and can't simply be willed into existence," wrote Satell in 2019. "It can only happen when people truly internalize and embrace it. The best way to do that is to empower those who already believe in change to bring in those around them."[52]

The case studies mentioned in the past few pages support this point. Top-down mandates pushed Disney to create an accessible park. Nike's company-wide product strategy led to the launch of an accessible shoe. However, the spread of consumer interest and demand made the commercial appeal for those innovations. People buy Nike shoes because they see others wearing them. People keep coming to Disney Shanghai because they know others had a great experience there.

Change happens organically – or side-by-side – to use Satell's terminology. Satell has published several articles and books that powerfully argue that change does not occur by convincing people or using momentous kick-off events with celebrities to spur enthusiasm. As Satell wrote, "... a better strategy is to start by identifying your apostles – people who are already excited about the possibilities for change ... However, once you've identified your apostles, you can empower them to bring in others around them. Unlike top-down or bottom-up efforts, people generally have a pretty good idea which of their peers may be receptive."

Research on how ideas, goods, and services gain the public's attention has found that a single "influencer" (such as a Kardashian) or a significant event (such as a glitzy product launch) has limited impact in convincing people to support the idea or buy the product or service. For example, a team of academics and researchers at Yahoo! found that ideas on Twitter grow and content is shared in a peer-to-peer, word-of-mouth manner "via many small cascades, mostly triggered by ordinary individuals." Thus, ideas spread informally through networks of friends and peers because that is who people most trust.[53]

An August 2024 article in *MIT Sloan Management Review* validates the Yahoo! research conclusions. The authors of the *MIT Sloan Management Review* article analyzed several research papers about the reach and impact of so-called "nano influencers" – individuals with a relatively small but passionate following versus the "macro influencers" – those like Kim Kardashian – who have a large, global network of followers. Nano influencers are found to be both more cost-effective and able to generate a higher conversion rate on sales than macro influencers. The reason is the nano influencers cultivate relationships of trust with their network. Many people in the networks are aligned with the influencer through shared interests and background and, unlike global personalities, the nano influencers often engage directly with their network, furthering the closeness in the relationship.[54]

In other words, an ad featuring a famous person may get you interested in a product. But the recommendation of the people you most trust – friends, neighbors, and family – often decides whether you buy it.

The truth is that small groups that are loosely connected but united in a common purpose are how we drive change and transformation. Kim Kardashian has millions of followers, but she has never transformed anything. Her behavior has influenced no outcome of consequence. She may impact purchasing decisions or the look of someone's wardrobe. But that is the extent of her influence.

Now, think back to Blackwell's concept of the curb-cut effect. To make lasting change, small groups of people came together and gradually broadened their networks of allies and supporters. Yes, curb cuts took far too long to become part of the architecture of our communities. However, it happened, and there is no going backward. Archer's Challenge spread because he was known within his school and community. People knew Archer was doing something significant with his challenge, and they trusted him to turn the challenge into meaningful results.

That theory of change plays directly into the strengths of the global disability community. The disability community is a loosely connected but passionate network of people and organizations willing to apply their ideas, voices, and money to improve the world. Because of their shared life experiences, there is an inherent level of trust among many in the disability community.

Viewed that way, the ability to use disability-driven innovation to achieve the systemic change needed to create an accessible, inclusive, and universally equitable society is doable. Governments can't mandate inclusion and equity. Companies can't make perfect markets that accept everyone equally. And none of us can trigger the curb-cut effect alone. However, working as a network of trusted voices, collaborators, early adopters, and partners, the disability community can apply its sense of urgency and passion for innovation to transform society for the better.

Case Study: Not Every Curb Cut Is Identical

Giorgi Dzneladze has been a disability rights advocate for over 30 years. He pioneered the disability movement in Georgia in the early 1990s. Since then, Giorgi has been at the forefront of advancing the rights, employment opportunities, and accessibility of persons with disabilities. One of his most outstanding achievements is spearheading the passage of Georgia's disability rights law, national disability rights action plans, and standards and programs of social services that serve persons with disabilities.

Giorgi has been a wheelchair user since 1975 and founded the Georgian Wheelchair Workshop – a social enterprise that produces assistive technologies for persons with disabilities. Giorgi has designed and built thousands of wheelchairs for people all over the world, all of them customized for the user's specific needs.

The first wheelchair models were manual, but within six years, the Georgian Wheelchair Workshop was producing powered versions. Today's wheelchairs are rugged yet lightweight, stable but comfortable, and controlled by high-end electronics.

The differentiator of the wheelchairs designed and built by Giorgi and his team is their adaptability in every situation. His wheelchairs are innovated and built for universal use, anywhere in the world. As Giorgi said, "With a wheelchair, you should be able to access anything – nature, streets, museums, buses, airports, and airplanes. If a wheelchair can't take you where you want to go, it limits you as a person."

The problem is that many wheelchairs are not designed and built for universal use. For example, even the most advanced and modern wheelchairs made in the United States do not work well in Georgia. In inaccessible environments, navigating with these wheelchair models is nearly impossible. Ramps, curb cuts, and building entrances are different in the two countries. What works just fine in America or Northern Europe does not work in Georgia.

Giorgi has a powerful lesson for disability-driven innovation – mass production to reach a global market is not always the best solution. Instead, innovators must find a way to customize their goods and services to the individual. Failure to do so leads to products that do not fully meet the needs of each person given the environment in which they live and work. "True innovation happens when you create a tailored solution for each person. Yes, I sell a lot of wheelchairs to people around the world. But each wheelchair is designed specifically for that person and what they need to live a better, more productive life. If I just mass-produced wheelchairs with no consideration for the person, I would not be innovating. I would just be manufacturing."[55]

Although the curb cut effect is real, it is essential to remember that many curb cuts are different. That fact must always be front and center as we seek to innovate a better world.

CHAPTER 3

Understanding and Appreciating Disability

So, it's important to remember that if you've met one disabled person, you've met one disabled person. And if you have a disability, then the only disability experience you are an expert on is your own.

—Emily Ladau, disability rights activist and author

The most fundamental thing about disability is that it's intersectional. That means it cuts across every trait that defines us as human beings – ethnicity, gender, sexual orientation, religious affiliation, socio-economic status, and geographic location, to name just a few.

It is an irrefutable fact that every one of us will experience disability in our lives. Some of us are born with a disability; others become disabled due to a life experience such as an auto accident or emotional trauma. Unless we discover the fountain of youth, we all face the reality of aging and experiencing physical and cognitive limitations as we age. Simply put, "The disability community is the only minority group that anyone can join at any time."[56]

Disability can be permanent, or it can be temporary. If you fall off a bike and break your arm, you are disabled until your arm heals. Disabilities can be apparent, or they can be hidden. Depression and anxiety are forms of disabilities, just as limitations in mobility, vision, and hearing.

Disability can also be situational. These are disabilities that occur due to a specific, short-term circumstance. An example is a parent holding an infant child in one arm while trying to fill out an intake form at a pediatrician's office with the other.

Beyond our conditions of disability, we frequently encounter disability through our network of friends and families. Each of us has served as a caregiver to someone with a disability – be it nursing a child back to health after a playground injury, helping a neighbor who has a chronic illness, or caring for an elderly parent with dementia.

The Americans with Disabilities Act (ADA) – the landmark 1990 civil rights law establishing legal protections for persons with disabilities – formalized the definition of disability. Granted, the ADA applies only to the United States. However, it has served as a model for similar civil rights laws in other countries, and thus, its approach and mindset to defining disability are broadly applicable.

According to the ADA, the term "disability" means a person with:

- A physical or mental impairment that substantially limits one or more of the major life activities of such individual;

- A record of such an impairment; or

- Being regarded as having such an impairment[57]

According to the ADA National Network, a U.S.-based resource for implementing the ADA in professional environments, being "regarded as" disabled means that the person either:

- Has an impairment that does not substantially limit a major life activity;

- Has an impairment that substantially limits a major life activity only as a result of the attitudes of others toward them; or

- Does not have any impairment but is treated by an entity as having an impairment.[58]

Within these broad definitions of disability, there are established criteria that more specifically detail types of disabilities. Disabled World has identified "8 main types of disability" that encompass both its visible and invisible traits along with environmental factors that impact how we live:[59]

1. Mobility/Physical – limitations in movement, dexterity, or coordination

2. Spinal Cord – dysfunctioning of the sensory organizations due to injury to the spinal cord

3. Head Injuries – there are two types of brain injuries:

   - Acquired Brain Injury (ABI) – a degeneration of the brain that occurs after birth

   - Traumatic Brain Injury - caused by a forceful bump, blow, or jolt to the head or body, or from an object that pierces the skull and enters the brain[60]

4. Vision – impairments ranging from blindness to diabetes-related eye conditions

5. Hearing – full or partial deafness

6. Cognitive or Learning – impairments that present learning difficulties for people, such as dyslexia, intellectual deficits, or dementia

7. Psychological Disorders – disabilities related to the mood or feeling states of a person, such as anxiety, depression, post-traumatic disorder (PTSD), and eating disorders such as anorexia

8. Invisible Disabilities – conditions that are not immediately apparent to others, such as Crohn's disease and sleep disorders

The precision of these definitions is helpful to understanding the nuances of disabilities because simplified descriptions of disability can be deceptive. For example, the international symbol of disability is an icon of a wheelchair user – an image that conveys a static, permanent, and obvious disability. That icon also misinterprets the nature of disability – people are wheelchair users, not wheelchair-bound. The reality is that more than 90 percent of disabilities are invisible. Conditions of disability can vary from day to day. Stress levels and weather changes can impact the mood of a person with depression.

Simple definitions of disability do not always convey that disability occurs across a spectrum. A mobility limitation in one leg is a less severe disability than using a prosthetic device. Relying on a hearing aid to compensate for a partial hearing loss differs from complete deafness. Chronic depression can be more severe than seasonal affective disorder. People also experience disability in different ways. For example, people with severe migraines can have differing triggers, levels of discomfort, and duration of symptoms.

The expansive definition of disability further reinforces its intersectional nature and the proximity of disability to our lives. Disability's often-hidden nature reminds us that any person at any point in time could experience it without anyone else knowing about it. Many of us may be experiencing a disability without full awareness of how the condition manifests itself in our bodies. Instead of treating disability as a static condition, appreciate that disability – and, by extension, the disability community – is dynamic, varied, and in a constant state of evolution.

Further, there often are unexpected causes of widespread disability across society. The rapid spread of AIDS in the 1980s led to millions of deaths and millions more with physical impairments such as weakened immune systems. In January 2020, nearly all of us were blissfully unaware of the coming COVID-19 pandemic. We had no idea about what was to unfold in the coming months. Years later, the worst of the transmission phase of the pandemic is behind us. Yet, we continue to grapple with its aftershocks such as PTSD, depression, and anxiety triggered by isolation and the complex symptoms of "long COVID." If you did not have moments of depression or anxiety during March and April 2020, count yourself among the very few and the very lucky.

Given that every one of us encounters disability at some point, prominent activist and author Emily Ladau has offered a good suggestion – permanently strike the concept of "normal human function" from our lexicon. As Ladau asserts, the "normal" standard of function does not exist: "There's no need to create this kind of divide between non-disabled people and disabled people, or between people who have different disabilities because everyone functions differently. Instead, it's better to speak openly and directly about needs, abilities, and disabilities."[61]

Case Study: The Convention on the Rights of Persons with Disabilities: An Innovation that Transformed the United Nations

The Convention on the Rights of Persons with Disabilities (CRPD) was adopted by consensus at the United Nations General Assembly on December 13, 2006, and went into effect on May 3, 2008. The CRPD is notable for two reasons. The CRPD is the first international, legally binding instrument to set minimum standards for the rights of people with disabilities. In basic terms, the CRPD is the ADA on a global scale. Second, the CRPD transformed the United Nations (UN).

According to Allison Aslan of the U.S. State Department and former advisor to Judy Heumann:

By nature, you are going to be lost in the waves if you're just one voice or one type of disability group advocating for a specific need. But bringing together the voices of the entire disability community brought power and evidence of the far-reaching effects such a treaty would have. That powerful voice, unified in many ways, but also vastly diverse in content, was recognized. It was loud enough that the drafters included all these people in the consultation process. Using that collaboration to make change is disability innovation.

The Convention on the Rights of Persons with Disabilities (CRPD) was groundbreaking for its influence on the way state parties develop and implement policies affecting persons with disabilities. Persons with disabilities were not just consulted in the drafting of this treaty, they played a leading role in drafting it. Persons with disabilities were meaningfully included and sought out for their input. All kinds of persons with disabilities were represented in this process, not just persons who have a physical disability, or who have a disability and have a law degree to understand legal implications. During the development of this treaty, there was an intentional effort to reach out to as many segments of the disability community to make sure they were a part of the drafting of the CRPD. Often persons with developmental disabilities are left out [or the views of some groups are unfairly prioritized]. In this case, the consultation was able to reach globally to seek input from organizations of persons with disabilities of all kinds.

That practice of inclusion and bringing in people with lived experiences, not just educated experts who may or may not be members of the community of focus, is now standard practice at the UN. The UN now brings self-advocates and people who are the target of a policy, event, or program to be at the design and consultation tables. It's now the way the UN does business, and critical to that was the disability movement around the drafting of the CRPD.[62]

The Disparities of Disability

Disability does not affect people or communities equally. Wealthier Western communities tend to – but not consistently – implement greater accessibility features in their infrastructure, invest more in developing equitable education, and have better-resourced local organizations dedicated to advancing a more inclusive society. There also are sharp differences according to personal backgrounds. The systemic challenges encountered by the disability community are pervasive and immense, and even more so when viewed through intersectional lenses such as gender, sexual expression and identity, and race. According to Dikko Yusuf of the World Institute on Disability, "Marginalized people with disabilities are those who, in addition to being disabled, belong to another marginalized group. This includes those who belong to marginalized genders, races, ethnicities, sexualities, and/or economic backgrounds."[63]

When disability is examined through an intersectional perspective, an important distinction becomes clear. There is disability as a natural part of the human condition. Then, there are disability-related disparities that lead to sub-optimal socio-economic outcomes, such as less access to quality health care, biased hiring processes, housing discrimination, and inaccessible transportation. Many of those disability-related disparities are more acutely felt by populations such as women, minorities, the LGTBQ community, and people living in poor, underserved regions.

Compounding these inequities, global crises such as losses of healthy environmental ecosystems, extreme temperatures, and destructive weather events already put vulnerable populations at even greater risk.

The disabled population's challenges are gradual (rising sea levels and increasing air pollution) and sudden (floods, hurricanes, and fires). "Climate harm disproportionately impacts persons with disabilities because of their socioeconomic marginalization and invisibility within government and civil society at large," observed several Harvard Law School authors in a 2023 article in *Nature*. "In climate emergencies, persons with disabilities are excluded from disaster, health, and humanitarian services. Slow-onset climate change, such as sea level rise and hotter weather with subsequent water and food scarcity, amplifies existing exclusion and adds further barriers."[64]

Disability-Driven Innovation Is Not Monolithic

The pronounced differences across the disabled community and the disparate challenges faced by persons with disabilities only reinforce the dynamic and fluid nature of disability-driven innovation. Disability-driven innovation occurs across every market in the global economy and is often a direct outcome of an individual taking action to fix a problem in their everyday life.

Too often, we equate innovation with technological advances backed by prominent investors at venture capital firms based in Silicon Valley, California. In reality, innovation – particularly disability-driven innovation – takes many forms. At its core, disability-driven innovation is necessary for people trying to adapt to a world that is not accessible or inclusive. Em Hillman innovated the idea of a coffee shop in Independence, Iowa, because running her own business best fit her skills, and she did not want to work in a sheltered workshop. Although the typewriter's exact origins are challenging to discern, one of its earliest iterations was created by an Italian – Pellegrino Turri, who, in the early 1800s, built a typewriter-like device for his blind lover Countess Fantoni da Fivizzano so they could communicate.[65]

A critical difference between disability-driven innovation and commonly held perceptions of innovation is that a significant amount of innovation occurs in the so-called "informal economy." Most of us operate in the "formal economy," governed by laws, subject to forms of taxation, conventional methods of buying and selling goods and services, and established protections for workers and innovators.

In contrast, the informal economy operates outside traditional norms and practices. It is the difference between shopping at a Walmart or Carrefour versus street vendors. Or working at an innovation lab of a global tech company instead of a workshop in a garage.

According to the International Labour Organization (ILO), "The informal economy refers to all economic activities by workers and economic units that are – in law or practice – not covered or insufficiently covered by formal arrangements. It thrives mostly in a context of high unemployment, underemployment, poverty, gender inequality, and precarious work."[66] Not by coincidence, each of those traits is often synonymous with disability.

Its scale is vast – about 2 billion people work in the informal economy worldwide. That represents 60 percent of the global workforce. While its size varies by region and country, the ILO estimates that the informal economy contributes roughly 15 percent of the gross domestic product (GDP) in northern and western economies and 35 percent in less developed economies. For example, the informal economy provides nearly 86 percent of employment in Africa and almost 70 percent in Asia and the Arab states. In contrast, it provides 40 percent of jobs in the Americas and 25 percent in Europe.

In a 2022 study for the ILO, Tendy Gunawan and Jahen Rezki found that approximately 78 percent of persons with severe disabilities and 76 percent of persons with mild disabilities are employed in the global informal economy.[67] A 2021 World Bank study found that persons with disabilities in Latin America are 11 times more likely than non-disabled persons to be in the informal economy.[68] Given the preponderance of people with disabilities in the informal economy and the reality that marginalized populations usually cannot access traditional approaches to innovation, it makes perfect sense that innovation by persons with disabilities mirrors that of the informal economy.

In the informal economy, innovation often results from having less, not more. Development and design processes are low-cost, agile, and organic. Meeting immediate and basic human needs is the driving force rather than a desire to change the world or become the next Elon Musk or Steve Jobs.[69]

Brian Mwenda, the founder and CEO of Hope Tech, an organization focused on innovating solutions for the visually impaired, made a significant distinction between innovation in developing and developed countries. "When I look at developing countries in Kenya and East Africa, disability innovation is driven by a need for economic support," noted Mwenda. "Things like going back to work or starting a business entrepreneurship. Most people with disabilities are looking for assistive devices and innovation to help them become economically self-reliant, provide for their families, and provide for themselves. That is largely because there isn't a lot of government support in this area."

"But when you look at countries in Europe, there's a lot of government support. Innovation in those countries is much more driven towards social outcomes. Enabling people to do things socially more than doing things out of economic need."[70]

For all of us committed to advancing disability-driven innovation, the challenge is understanding and enabling it in all its forms so that it quickly scales into broader adoption and use across the economy.

Case Study: JT FireStarters: Innovation at the Intersection of Employment and the Circular Economy

As our world faces the challenges of resource scarcity, climate change, pollution, and spiraling costs of materials, many believe the circular economy is the only way the free-market economy will sustain itself. The Ellen MacArthur Foundation provides a helpful description of how to envision the circular economy compared to today's economy: "The circular economy takes a different approach [than traditional forms of production]. Instead of allowing valuable materials to go to waste and natural systems to be degraded, it applies three principles: eliminate waste and pollution, circulate products and materials, and regenerate nature. This means designing buildings, cars, and electronics, for instance, to be used longer, reused many times, remanufactured, and, in the end, recycled. This keeps the resources that went into making them – the materials, energy, and people's time – in the economy."[71]

While we are nowhere close to achieving the circular economy on that level, companies worldwide are trying to make it happen – and spending more than $1.3 trillion in the process. Much of the cost is driven by companies belatedly retrofitting circular processes onto existing means of operations and production.[72]

In contrast, JT FireStarters was innovated from Day 1 to embrace the circular economy. Launched in 2015 by Daniel Toops and his family in the small town of Peosta, Iowa (U.S.), JT FireStarters makes packages of shredded paper, cardboard egg cartons, and wax from unused candles that are used to start a fire in a fireplace, a grill, or at a camping site. One customer wrote on the JT FireStarters' website, "We go camping almost every weekend and always enjoy sitting around a campfire. These fire starters are the quickest and easiest way to get a fire started even when it is damp outside. Just one fire starter and some kindling and we are ready to roast marshmallows in a matter of minutes."

Despite the positive reviews, Daniel and his family did not launch JT FireStarters because they were passionate about helping people enjoy their time around a campfire while roasting marshmallows.

When Daniel was 14, he and his parents met with a large team of school administrators to discuss his educational and career plans. Daniel's autism and obsessive-compulsive disorder (OCD) meant that a traditional path through school was no longer viable. Unfortunately, no one from his school in that meeting – or in any meeting after that – had any good suggestions for Daniel's career.

With no ideas forthcoming, Daniel's parents started exploring other options for him. Enrolling in a sheltered workshop was not feasible because most in his area had closed or faced uncertain futures. Plus, the family wanted the challenge of starting a business.

Daniel's first attempt at entrepreneurship was making laundry detergent packets. That proved to be unworkable. Making fleece blankets was next. But Daniel did not like being in the blanket business.

The third attempt was fire starters. Daniel quickly came to enjoy making fire starters because the process involves multiple steps, all of which must be done precisely and sequentially. This plays to Daniel's strengths as someone with autism and OCD.

Furthermore, the business has a meager budget because Daniel embraces circular production methods. JT FireStarters rarely buys materials. All the lint, paper, egg cartons, and wax are donated by people or organizations in and around Peosta that want to recycle those materials rather than send them to a landfill as waste.

JT FireStarters enjoys a strong support community – the all-important social capital that is the lifeblood of entrepreneurs. Daniel's mom, Katherine, designed a step-by-step process for Daniel to follow in making the fire starters. She is also the face of the company, as Daniel is non-verbal. Daniel's dad built some of the tools used in the shop to expedite production. He is also ready to lend a hand in production when orders pile up. A group of Daniel's teachers and friends reached out to their networks in the community to begin sourcing the materials Daniel needed to make the fire starters. JT FireStarters was also supported by the business development specialists at Iowa Vocational Rehabilitation Services' Self Employment Program.

"This is how a business is supposed to work," said Katherine Toops. "It is a special connection between the home, the community, and customers. I wish I could say this was the typical way things happen, but I don't think it is."[73]

More than furthering the circular economy, Daniel is furthering the local economy. Because of its continued growth in sales, JT FireStarters has two additional employees, both of whom identify as disabled. As Katherine Toops said, "In these uncertain times, our family is determined to remain committed to help Daniel and his co-workers continue to 'Start Something Good' – which is our tagline – and grow the business so more people with disabilities can have meaningful employment that is accommodating to individual needs."

The Disability's Diversity Is Good for Innovation

As noted in Chapter 1, there is a strong business case for hiring talent with disabilities and empowering them across an organization. Just because an organization commits to a more diverse and inclusive workforce does not mean it will suddenly unleash a torrent of innovation. Instead, innovation comes from bringing together people's various lived experiences and allowing them to collaborate. It also means that the tools and resources employees use in their work must be universally designed and accessible to all – something we will cover later in the book.

However, the payoff is monumental if an organization can establish a strong foundation for innovation. As Keely Cat-Wells said, "The more lived experiences and the more diversity you bring together, the more people that you will reach, the more people that you will impact positively, and the more customers you will have. You get things that you've never seen or that have never been built before. Rather than working in silos or with small groups of people who have similar experiences, you get thinking that is outside that box, it is global, and you are bringing in people that otherwise may not have a chance to contribute. Because of that, you get the most incredible array of perspectives and innovation."[74]

As is apparent from Cat-Well's statement, the most significant driver of disability-driven market opportunity is disability's intersectional nature. Because disability cuts across all our traits as humans, we all have different lived experiences, perspectives, and ideas for how to innovate. Some of us are great at coming up with "pie in the sky" ideas. Others are talented at turning those ideas into tangible goods or services. Still others are best suited to marketing those goods and services to potential customers.

We must appreciate that disability-driven innovation is not monolithic and applies differently to all of us. We must be careful not to impose an innovation on someone just because it is a new, seemingly better, more cost-efficient product compared to other options on the market. Joe Quintanilla, the Vice President of Development and Major Gifts at National Braille Press made an important point when explaining the risks of imposing an innovation on students with visual disabilities. "I hear this a lot from parents. Some school systems will say to the parent or the student, 'Here's an iPad, and you can listen to your books and use it to navigate your schoolwork." I know that an iPad is a great innovation, and it helps a lot of people learn. But there is a deficit here. Because now you're asking, or maybe even forcing, a kid to be an auditory learner versus a reading learner by using books printed in Braille."[75]

Case Study: Innovative Partnerships to Create Career Opportunities

Down Syndrome Innovations (DSI) is a non-profit organization that provides support services to persons with Down syndrome and their families. A significant focus of Down Syndrome Innovations is creating employment opportunities in the greater Kansas City (U.S.) region for persons with Down syndrome.

In 2021, Down Syndrome Innovations launched a partnership with the Kansas City Chiefs, one of the most iconic and successful teams in the National Football League, to provide game-day jobs for individuals with Down syndrome. The partnership's starting point was to hire individuals into Guest Service Representative positions in the club-level suites at each of the Chiefs' home games.

The collaboration began in mid-season 2021 when the Chiefs needed staff to help greet and scan tickets of guests entering the stadium. The Chiefs reached out to Amanda Myers, the Employment Coordination for DSI, to determine if people in their network were available to work the games. The Chiefs brought on two hires from DSI, plus Myers, who served as their job coach.

After that small start, the partnership grew quickly – going far beyond the Chiefs. As Myers explained, "It started with just me job coaching two people at Arrowhead Stadium. Then, it evolved into 12 people the next year and 18 the next season and we started expanding into other game day roles, including positions on the environmental team."

"We then took the same blueprint to the Royals [Kansas City's Major League baseball team]. We showed them the partnership with the Chiefs, and then the Royals wanted to be part of it. The Royals hired 16 people in their first season across a variety of departments. We learned that the club level was where people were most successful because the space was indoors and some of the employees had previous experience working with individuals with diverse abilities."

Myers continued, "Since 81 home games would've been challenging to schedule, we developed a system where individuals chose days of the week to work. Now the Kansas City Current [Kansas City's National Women's Soccer League team] also has a few individuals from DSI working at their games. We've learned that it's helpful to use a phased approach by training small groups of individuals at a time, instead of trying to train a large group at once or needing to provide one-on-one job coaching to everyone."

Jack Anderson, who manages the Royals' partnership for DSI, said, "Hiring inclusively has changed the staff culture. Other Major League Baseball teams have started talking to us about our program because they want to hire individuals with diverse abilities. These partnerships embody the strengths-based approach to customized employment. We work really hard to ensure that all staff are in positions that match their skill set. These customized jobs have also created capacity-building opportunities, where staff are freed up to work at the highest scope of their role."

Anderson's comment alludes to a significant outcome of DSI's work with the Chiefs, Royals, and Current – the ability to scale the employment model with other professional sports organizations. "It's been amazing to see what can happen by just getting your foot in the door and then see how an idea can grow," said Myers. "It is important that employers are talking to employers because they learn a lot from each other. And we have developed a blueprint that anyone else can use. These systems can be replicated and improved over time."

For the staff, working with a major professional sports team is a once-in-a-lifetime opportunity to obtain lasting career skills and build a resume for other employment opportunities. While the positions staffed by the DSI members are entry-level, they are similar to the entry-level positions many of us had when we were young. The positions allow for advancement in the organizations, and there is an expectation that each person becomes increasingly independent over their tenure.

Despite the rapid success of the DSI partnerships with the Kansas City-area sports teams, there were initial challenges and many lessons learned. Myers has noted some of them:

- Start small. It is much more important to have early success than to launch the partnership with many staff playing an extensive role at the athletic venues. This allows you to refine processes and work through logistics on a smaller scale, and then you can grow over time once you've identified what works best and is sustainable.

- Set everyone up for success. Understand the individuals you're serving and their support staff. It is essential to spend time getting to know people's strengths, preferences, and how they learn best. It's also crucial to train the staff on how to keep individuals focused on their work and support them during transition times. We've conducted training for several employers on how to work with individuals with diverse abilities and then more in-depth training with the coworkers they'll be working with every game. Our individuals fill out an "All About Me" form that is shared with the employer so they have "bios" on everyone. We found that, when employers are equipped with a practical toolkit, they are more comfortable supporting individuals with diverse abilities in the workplace and rely less on our DSI staff for support.

- It is a career path, not a job. "Everyone deserves the opportunity to have career advancement," said Myers. "If you think about any of our employment journeys, many of our first jobs were in the hospitality industry, and many of us are in different roles now than we were when we first started. You learn a lot of lessons from each job you have, that you then take those to the next job and the job after that. We also know it's all about who you know. These work experiences provide individuals with opportunities to network with others in their community, which could lead to another job in the future. If one of the seasonal jobs goes well then, we help them find permanent employment in a similar industry. In addition to these sporting work experience opportunities, individuals typically have another part-time permanent position with another employer."

- Allow people to take on growing responsibilities. Now that the partnerships have been running for a few years, several staff members are developing their positions. For example, some serve in a leadership role and train the new staff. Myers has even hired individuals with diverse abilities as job coaches because she found people learn well from someone who has similar experiences.

- Always be learning. Every season brings new challenges and new opportunities to expand the staff's roles. Amanda Myers and her team are constantly adapting the day-to-day work of the partnerships so that improvements are continuous. As Myers said, "You figure it out as you go. It is trial and error, so you can see what works best for that employer. Then, you can put more structures and systems in place to make the model sustainable. Every employer is different, every person is different, but you can take a framework and tweak it to what works best for your organization."

Another critical aspect of the partnerships between DSI and the sports teams is that the staff performance is evaluated, just as any other person in a similar role. The teams partnering with DSI want to foster a more inclusive environment for fans and employees alike. "They are expected to perform just like everyone else," noted Myers. "Those working with the Kansas City Chiefs get evaluated alongside all other personnel serving in similar positions at the end of the year. Short-term work experiences set the employer and individual up for success because if it's not the best fit, it has a natural end to it, and we can find something different for them."

The DSI team has created long-term value throughout the Chiefs' organizations by bringing their different lived experiences to the job. As Caitlin Pettit, the Director of Event Services for the Chiefs, remarked, "Hiring employees with diverse abilities has provided opportunities for ongoing education for managers and those in leadership roles. It has opened the eyes of many staff members who may have assumed that staff members with different abilities wouldn't thrive in roles that they are now excelling in."

The Royals are reaping the rewards of the partnership with DSI. "This partnership created a win-win situation: the individuals gained valuable experience while significantly enhancing our team and the guest experience," said Jarrett Alley, Assistant Manager of Ballpark Services for the Royals. "We ranked among the best teams in [Major League

Baseball] for guest satisfaction, and the DSI group was instrumental in achieving that recognition."

Amanda Myers is candid about her hopes for the future of the partnerships, "It's my dream that when we get a call from another sports team, we can tell them, 'Here's the blueprint. Take it. Learn from what we've done over the past few years. Then refine it and mobilize a partnership with an employment provider in your area.' That way we can impact the entire nation, not just Kansas City."[76]

CHAPTER 4

The Disability Employment and Innovation Landscape

Owning all the responsibilities of becoming a disability-inclusive organization is an enormous opportunity for employers to enrich the way they do business and cultivate a trustworthy culture among their employees.
—Cara Elizabeth Yar Khan, CEO, The Purple Practice

Despite the pervasive nature of disability across the economy, disabled people across the world face structural hurdles that limit their full participation in the workforce. The hurdles impact every person with a disability seeking employment – employees or self-employed entrepreneurs. As we will cover, these barriers also stifle the innovative potential of persons with disabilities, regardless of their employment status.

Millions of disabled people turn to self-employment because traditional employment – such as a 9-5 job, working for an established organization – does not fit their skills and needs. Millions of others are not allowed to participate in traditional employment due to discriminatory or inaccessible hiring practices.

It is no coincidence that, according to the United Nations, "In developing countries, 80 to 90 percent of persons with disabilities of working age are unemployed, whereas in industrialized countries, the figure is between 50 percent and 70 percent."[77] In the United States, the unemployment rate for persons with disabilities is generally around 7 to 8 percent, depending on broader economic conditions.[78] However, that number is wildly inaccurate. It only represents disabled persons who consider themselves in the workforce tied to the formal economy or actively seeking work in the formal economy. The reality is much more problematic. According to the U.S. Department of Labor's Bureau of Labor Statistics, "In 2022, 21.3 percent of persons with a disability were employed, up from 19.1 percent in 2021."[79]

In other words, nearly 80 percent of the working-age disabled population is either outside the workforce or participating in the informal economy as a means of earning a living. Neither outcome is ideal – millions of unemployed persons with disabilities are not in the workforce because they cannot find fulfilling employment or work informally, thus potentially lacking basic workplace legal protections, access to employer-sponsored health care, retirement benefits, etc. In contrast, the U.S. Department of Labor found that "For persons without a disability, 65.4 percent were employed" in the mainstream economy.[80]

Disability's intersectional nature permeates the global employment status of the population with disabilities – regardless of the nature of employment. There is more variability and nuance in understanding the employment and socio-economic status of the disabled population as compared to the population not currently experiencing a disability. As we will explore in this chapter, there are significant differences among employment opportunities, compensation, public benefits, types of jobs, and job security based not just on a person's disability but also on determinants such as age, geographic location, gender, access to vocational rehabilitation programs, and education.

For example, the United States does not provide a supplemental allowance to persons with disabilities to help offset the costs of a disability – such as repairs to a wheelchair or accessibility modifications to a residence. According to the National Disability Institute, shortcoming is an outlier in the Western world as many countries, including the United Kingdom and Sweden, provide such assistance.[81]

Consider the wide variability in vocational rehabilitation programs – government- administered programs designed to provide persons with disabilities with the resources and training to enter the workforce and enjoy career mobility. The U.S. system tends to prioritize competitive, integrated employment with an emphasis on securing jobs rather than creating long-term careers. Although the U.S. vocational rehabilitation system is backed by ample government funding at the federal and state levels, the system is fragmented, with high degrees of variability in how states administer programs. In many cases, state and federal employment programs are hampered by overly complex eligibility guidelines.

In contrast, many Western European countries and Japan are understood to have a more streamlined approach to using vocational rehabilitation initiatives to bring disabled people into the workforce. Very few developing countries, unfortunately, have robust vocational rehabilitation systems. Instead, they rely on a patchwork of assistance ranging from services provided by NGOs operating in local communities to global organizations like the United Nations and the International Labour Organization.

Disability Disclosure versus Self-Identification

The most consequential way a person with a disability interacts with anyone in the workforce – be they a colleague, employer, business partner, or potential client, to name just a few – is through their decision to share (or not share) their disability. There is no right or wrong approach to communicating a disability. It is a deeply personal choice with legal, social, cultural, and economic implications.

The University of Massachusetts Chan Medical School has developed a helpful distinction between the two ways people communicate their disability status in the workplace:

1. Disclosure – when an employee discloses information about their disability to their employer while requesting an accommodation needed to perform the essential functions of their job successfully.

2. Self-Identification – when an employee voluntarily identifies themselves to their employer as a person with a disability either informally or in response to a formal request from the employer.[82]

A third option for a person with a disability to disclose their disability in the workplace (or in any setting, for that matter) is to make a public announcement. This step is purely personal and varies from person to person. As such, an announcement can take many forms, from direct, personal communications to social media platforms to reach a wider audience.

Another layer of complexity in the disclosure and identification process is those people who are not disabled but have a direct connection to a person with a disability. Examples include parents of children with disabilities, siblings, or caregivers. Each of these people may want to share their connection to disability publicly and, as part of that process, may seek a reasonable accommodation at work, such as a flexible schedule. Again, for persons with a connection to disability, the choice to disclose that connection is a personal decision.

The Americans with Disabilities Act "prohibits employers from retaliating against employees who file or participate in a disability discrimination claim. Employees and job applicants with disabilities are also protected against interference, meaning an employer cannot intermediate, coerce, or threaten an employee from exercising their ADA rights."

Just because the legal protections are in place does not mean the cultural and attitudinal protections also are in place. When asked why he did not disclose his blindness when applying for over 100 jobs early in his career, James Warnken, a legally blind digital accessibility specialist, entrepreneur, and consultant, gave a brutally honest admission:

It started in school. Kids are mean. Being in fourth grade and everybody having 8 ½ by 11 worksheets. And mine was 11 by 17. I was different. I had to go to a different classroom to take a test. It was a learned behavior because I can't see I'm different, and people have to do things differently in the work setting. That's terrifying. Because as the employer, that's your responsibility to make those accommodations a reasonable accommodation? What is in it for an employer to take on that additional responsibility when there are 30 other applications that they don't have to do? And that was my mindset. I'm competing with other people to show them why I am the best fit, why I will cause the least friction, why I will hit the ground running without needing as much onboarding or training.[83]

Or consider this statement from Mike Hess, a former six-figure-earning corporate consultant who founded the Blind Institute of Technology to address the rampant unemployment of persons with visual disabilities:

"Even after making it into corporate America and succeeding, there's this internal conversation in your head saying you don't deserve to be there."[84]

The delicate balance between the merits of self-disclosure to obtain reasonable accommodations in a workplace and the unease and risk that come with self-disclosure has put persons with disabilities in a lose-lose situation. On the one hand, employers need to get the benefits of every employee bringing their best, most authentic selves to work. On the other hand, employees with disabilities are struggling, both professionally and personally, and those struggles are weighing on many of them – and have weighed on them for a long time.

In a global survey of over 5,000 individuals, Accenture – the global consultancy – found that 76 percent of employees with disabilities do not fully disclose their disabilities at work (either formally through organizational channels such as a human resources department or informally to colleagues). There is much that goes into unpacking a person's motivations to disclose a disability. A critical factor in the low level of disclosure is that simply creating a mechanism by which employees can disclose a disability (such as an all-employee survey) does not mean that employees want to share their disability – or feel comfortable doing so.

Too often, organizations overly focus on disclosure and creating a sense of inclusion because they believe it is the right thing to do. The basic, albeit flawed, assumption is that persons with disabilities want to share their disability with others proactively. As a result, there is a genuine risk of unintentionally pressuring employees to disclose a disability (or a connection to disability), thus undermining well-intentioned efforts.

Research by Return on Disability (RoD) has found that many employees with disabilities do not feel comfortable disclosing a disability for fear of retribution by supervisors, being shunned by colleagues, or losing a chance for advancement. "In most cases, disclosures are made to immediate managers, who, alongside Human Resources and third-party healthcare providers, assess the request and provide the eventual accommodation," noted a 2023 RoD paper. "This model operates on the assumption that PWD will disclose their disabilities to management: often the individuals most directly responsible for their career advancement. For many PWD, this system provides a strong incentive not to disclose."[85]

This is a long way of explaining that organizations cannot expect employees to disclose their disabilities and use their disabilities to the benefit of their jobs unless there is an exceptionally strong culture in place. Self-disclosure only happens when employees believe the organization values their disabilities and lived experiences.

Breaking Down Barriers, Not Boundaries

The ambition is to create a culture that breaks down barriers that inhibit employees from performing well. We must be cautious not to take that goal too far and to a point where it starts to impose on personal boundaries. We need to create a space for people to feel comfortable in an environment where they unleash all their talents to create more innovative and impactful outcomes. Doing so will enable people to bring their <u>best selves</u> to the task. That does not mean people bring their <u>entire selves</u> to the task. There is not a single person on this planet who wants their co-workers, collaborators, investors, and everyone else to know every single thing about their lives. All of us have boundaries, and those must always be respected.

There is also a difference between barriers and boundaries regarding professional norms. Just because an organization has created a culture where the barriers to personal expression have been lowered does not mean that the people in the organization have permission to do or say anything they like. Making a statement praising Adolf Hitler is reprehensible no matter the circumstances – not to mention crossing the boundaries of acceptable behavior towards colleagues.

Within this context, the "psychological safety" concept is highly relevant. Rebecca Berry, a leadership coach and consultant, provides a helpful definition of psychological safety:

> *In a psychologically safe environment, people are comfortable taking risks such as sharing their opinions, admitting mistakes, asking 'stupid' questions, and suggesting new ideas. They feel comfortable because they know nobody is going to embarrass them or make fun of them. And (importantly) they know there will be no negative repercussions. In working environments with little or no psychological safety, people worry that saying the wrong thing or admitting to mistakes will get them into trouble, and maybe even harm their careers.*

Psychological safety is not static or identically experienced by everyone. Instead, it exists on a continuum. Timothy R. Clark, founder and CEO of LeaderFactor, a leadership consulting organization, wrote a book entitled *The 4 Stages of Psychological Safety: Defining the Path to Inclusion and Innovation,* in which he helps readers appreciate the nuances of psychological safety. Clark's four stages are:

1. Inclusion Safety – members feel safe to belong to the team. They are comfortable being present, do not feel excluded, and feel wanted and appreciated.

2. Learner Safety – members can learn by asking questions. Team members here may be able to experiment, make (and admit) small mistakes, and ask for help.

3. Contributor Safety – members feel safe to contribute their ideas without fear of embarrassment or ridicule. This is a more challenging state because volunteering your ideas can increase team members' psychosocial vulnerability.

4. Challenger Safety – members can question others' (including those in authority) ideas or suggest significant changes to ideas, plans, or ways of working. Challenger safety is an equal combination of establishing respect for all and granting permission for all to think outside the box.

According to Clark, innovation is unleashed only when a culture reaches Challenger Safety.

"In organizations, it's an uncontested finding that high psychological safety drives performance and innovation, while low psychological safety incurs the disabling costs of low productivity and high attrition," he wrote.

As proof, Clark cites research Google conducted on its culture. After studying 180 of its teams, Google found that "smarts and resources can't compensate for what a team may lack in psychological safety." The company landed on psychological safety as the single most important factor in explaining high performance.

Challenger Safety cannot be parsed out in pieces or employed on some days but not others. "... to scale innovation throughout an organization, leaders must establish a norm of challenging the status quo. No technology-enabled suggestion box or collaborative jam session will work without underlying challenger safety. And keep in mind that not responding to a suggestion can be worse than outright rejection – which is at least an acknowledgment."[86]

Image 3: The Four Stages of Psychological Safety

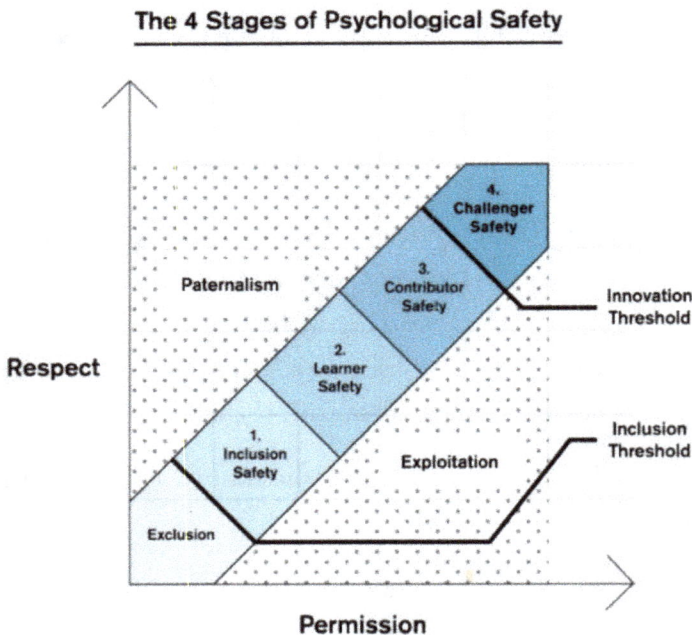

Image Description: A chart with the Y axis labeled "Respect" and the X axis labeled "Permission". A series of 5 blue boxes appear from the lower left to the upper right, with the top right area labeled "Challenger Safety". Source: The 4 Stages of Psychological Safety.

Clark's four stages do not only apply to corporate workplaces. They define every interaction we have as humans and every opportunity we are offered to innovate to make the world better.

It's one thing to collaborate for execution, which normally preserves the status quo. It's quite another to collaborate for innovation. Whereas execution is about creating value today, innovation is about creating value for tomorrow ... The process is not tidy, clean, or linear. It's messy and iterative. Imagination is the marriage of gnarly problems and creative chaos with the only process that you will produce something better.[87]

Remember that a disability-inclusive workforce has demonstrated a proven ability to create psychological safety for all employees. Creating psychological safety is not done for the benefit of the few. It is done for the benefit of all. Luisa Alemany and Freek Vermeulen, two professors at the London School of Business, surveyed 57 human resources professionals from companies worldwide that hired one or more people with a disability. Sixty-five percent of the respondents indicated that psychological safety had increased throughout their organizations since the hiring of employees who identify as disabled.[88]

Imagine a team of intrapreneurs at a multinational corporation with a great idea that addresses a major global issue. But when they pitch that idea to their boss, they aren't positioned to be their best selves in that interaction. The corporate culture is conformist and dominated by an attitude of "Get along to go along," and dismissing people who do not sufficiently toe the line is expected. New ideas are not prized but following orders is. The result is an idea that is stifled and never comes to fruition, to everyone's detriment.

The output from that team is sure to embody Henry Ford's famous quote, "If you always do what you've always done, you'll always get what you've always got."

Now, imagine those same people entering a space of psychological safety with their boss. The corporate culture prizes leaders who model effective leadership behaviors, such as openness, admitting mistakes, vulnerability, and encouraging respectful dialogues. Chances are they are pitching their idea as a cohesive team because collaboration is prized, and dismissing others is clearly not part of the culture. Their idea is likely to be bold and differentiated – critical traits for innovation – because that is what is expected.

This team's output will be different and norm-challenging. It will be driven by Brené Brown's observation that "Vulnerability is the birthplace of innovation, creativity, and change."

The bottom line is that innovation is just like respect. You can't buy it. You earn it – every day and through every action. Earning the ability to innovate successfully will require stepping out of comfort zones and considering different ways of interacting with people. Onboarding may need to change, meetings may have to be run differently, performance reviews must adapt and be more flexible, and much closer personal connections must be forged across the entire organization.

Consider how one small change by Hannah Bouline, the Director of Impact and Sustainability at Vertical Harvest, uncovered a better way of doing things. Located in Jackson, Wyoming (U.S.), Vertical Harvest is an innovator in vertical farming (growing plants and crops indoors and vertically through stacked rows rather than the traditional method of horizontal growing in open fields) and fostering competitive, integrated employment. As Bouline recounted,

> *I have this employee who is on the autism spectrum. She was a really strong employee but was having a lot of behavioral issues. Things would trigger her and she would walk out of work or meetings at work. We kept trying to talk to her but were getting nowhere. I was at this*

workshop, and someone suggested that we try non-verbal communication. So, we gave it a try. I would sit next to her, and we would each type our part of the conversation on a Google Sheet but on separate laptops. Just like an online chat. This nonverbal conversation was leaps and bounds better than anything we had been able to talk about before. We'd finally found her comfort zone. So, I started asking her, "You know, you walked out of work the other day. Why did you do that?" And her response was, "Well, the way we are doing things uses way more material and is more expensive. I was so frustrated we weren't doing things in the most efficient way possible."

My response was, "You gotta be kidding me. This is what is going on in your brain!" So now we know if we are going to have those kinds of breakthroughs, we need to make sure we are really communicating with the employees. It would have been really easy to make an assumption this was a bad employee and we needed to move on. It wasn't the case at all. This was a strong employee with a great idea to improve the company.[89]

The Medical vs Social Models of Disability Employment

Hannah Bouline's story is an essential lesson in understanding the nuances of how to bring out the best in disability employment and disability-driven innovation. While Disabled World has identified nearly 20 models used to understand and categorize the nature of disability,[90] the two most common are the medical and social models. The University of Oregon's (U.S.) Accessible Education Center provides a helpful distinction between the two:

- The Medical Model views disability as resulting from a person's physical or mental limitations and is not connected to the social or geographical environments. The Medical Model focuses on finding a "cure" or making a person more "normal."

- The Social Model views disability as a consequence of environmental, social, and attitudinal barriers that may prevent people from fully participating in society.[91]

Ashlea Lantz painted a sharp contrast between the two models regarding employment and innovation. "It's all about the mindset. Our society has operated on a mindset of disability being 'less than' or 'something being wrong with a disability.' We've relied on institutions and service systems that treat disability under the medical model. The focus has been on changing the person. However, disability-driven innovation treats disability with the mindset of the social model. It's about changing society so that we are more inclusive."[92]

In a November 2023 article in *MIT Sloan Management Review*, Maureen Dunne, a globally recognized neurodiversity expert, made a convincing case for using the mindset of the social model to not only embrace – but also maximize – the value-creating potential of neurodivergent employees:

No two neurodivergent people are the same, and it is important to value the richness and diversity of all kinds of minds, given that different individuals exhibit their own unique strengths and challenges. That said, there is a growing body of evidence that suggests that there is a correlation between different divergent neurotypes and uncommon skills, such as a heightened capacity for originality or innovative ideation. The results of numerous studies suggest that neurodivergent cognition is positively correlated with enhanced creativity and innovative thinking and that autistic people are less prone to cognitive biases and more consistent in making rational decisions than the general population. These unique perspectives and skills are inherently valuable to employers on an individual level while providing additional group-level value as a critical hedge against groupthink.[93]

If an organization wants to create a culture of psychological safety or a person wants to encourage psychological safety among their network of friends, embracing the social model of disability is a must. A person's medical condition is not the determining factor in how they contribute to innovation and human progress. Instead, we must embrace the social model of disability to create an inclusive society where talent is maximized.

The Economic Cost of Structural Unemployment of Persons with Disabilities

The failure to embrace a mindset of disability aligned with the social model has had severe and lasting consequences for every one of us – regardless of our disability status. Just as the medical model doesn't account for the barriers to employment by persons with disabilities, the exclusion of the population from the workforce is a barrier to more robust growth across the world's economy – to society's detriment.

Consider some of the following data that demonstrates bringing more disabled people into the global workforce has the potential to be massive and far-reaching:

The Center for American Progress – a Washington, DC-based think tank – estimates that, in the United States, "If disabled workers experienced the same employment rate as those without a disability, nearly 14 million more disabled people would have been employed in 2021."[94]

Each of those 14 million unemployed people represents missed revenue for local, state, and federal governments and, in many cases, additional costs to those governments through various public benefits programs. Instead of subsidizing people who are not working, our policies must be re-oriented towards encouraging and incentivizing willing workers to enter the workforce.

"We never talk about the hole created in our economy because people with disabilities are excluded from meaningful participation in the workforce," said Regina 'Gina' Kline. "It is not sustainable to treat people with disabilities as a charity and it benefits no one if people with disabilities aren't working."[95]

The facts support Kline's assertion. Consider the following:

- According to Accenture, the value of the U.S. economy could increase by $25 billion if just 1 percent more of the population with disabilities joined the workforce.[96]

- A 2019 study by the European Parliament Research Service determined that the loss of tax revenue in the European Union linked to lower educational attainment and employment levels was estimated to be 255€ to 416€ million per year (roughly $255 - $445 million per year). Furthermore, the loss of Gross Domestic Product (GDP) in the European Union was estimated at 710€ million to 1.2€ billion annually (roughly $760 million—$1.3 billion).[97]

- According to a paper by the United Nations Economic and Social Commission for Asia and the Pacific, "... increasing the economic participation of persons with disabilities and ensuring equal pay for persons with disabilities could augment gross domestic product by up to 7 percent."[98]

- In 2011, research by Deloitte found that, in Australia, "closing the gap between labor market participation rates and unemployment rates for people with and without disabilities by one-third would result in a cumulative $43 billion increase in Australia's GDP over the next decade in real dollar terms."[99] Because Australia failed to close the employment gap substantially since 2011, its economy underperformed by at least $43 billion – likely a conservative estimate given the underrepresented nature of disability.

- The World Bank found that the economic value of _unpaid_ caretaking work in Latin America ranges from 16 percent to 25 percent of GDP. To be clear – this is the measure of people working for free who could otherwise be contributing to the region's economy if they were compensated for their time and effort.[100] Finally, the World Bank provides a global perspective: "In economic terms alone, available global data suggest that the exclusion of people with disabilities represents a loss to countries of between 3 and 7 percent of GDP."[101]

While the burdens of economic underperformance are more often borne by the poor and marginalized, they impact every one of us regardless of socio-economic status or disability. As part of a global study on inequality, researchers at the United Nations noted that "High levels of inequality of opportunity discourage skills accumulation, choke economic and social mobility, and human development and, consequently, depress economic growth. It also entrenches uncertainty, vulnerability, and insecurity, undermines trust in institutions and government, increases social discord and tensions, and triggers violence and conflicts."[102]

Ultimately, "Those effects can take a chunk out of your paycheck, regardless of whether you're in the bottom 99 percent or the top 1 percent," observed Christopher Ingraham in a _Washington Post_ article.[103]

As economic performance at the macro level suffers when the disabled population is not fully employed, so does private sector performance. As a paper by Aaron De Smet and his colleagues at McKinsey & Company noted, "There is now a structural gap in the labor supply because there simply aren't enough traditional employees to fill all the openings. Even when employers successfully woo these workers from rivals, they are just reshuffling talent and contributing to wage escalation while failing to solve the underlying structural imbalance."[104]

Because too many companies are caught in a trap of reshuffling their talent, they need to take advantage of opportunities to diversify their talent pool in a way that spurs innovation. "It's time for companies to realize that the disability experience by definition is innovation personified," wrote Jonathan Kaufman, a consultant, psychotherapist, and academic with Cerebral Palsy. "Organizations have to think more broadly of what their current needs are and do a serious audit of the potential dividends that the disability experience can offer for future success."[105]

The pressing need to chase workplace talent has created a significant weakness in much of the private sector. With the innovation that comes from bringing together people of different lived experiences, companies can stay competitive, maintain market share with rivals, and maintain profitability and share price. Further, if the private sector is to play a meaningful role in addressing the myriads of existential threats we face today – climate change, extreme weather events, poverty, and lack of access to education are just a few examples – it makes no sense to be sidelining talent that has a centuries-long track record of innovation and problem-solving.

Conversely, those embracing diversity in all forms are winning the game. According to research by Boston Consulting Group, "The biggest takeaway we found is a strong and statistically significant correlation between the diversity of management teams and overall innovation. Companies that reported above-average diversity on their management teams also reported innovation revenue that was 19 percentage points higher than those with below-average leadership diversity – 45 percent of total revenue versus just 26 percent."[106]

Case Study: Disclo: Transforming the Workplace Accommodations Experience

Born at the intersection of market opportunity, gaps in traditional human resources (HR) processes, and unprecedented changes in how we work, Disclo's mission is to make the workplace accommodations process as seamless and transparent as possible for both employees and employers.

Led by its founder and CEO, Hannah Olson, Disclo is an HR tech software company helping employees to safely disclose and ask for accommodations at work. Hannah's passion for improving the workplace accommodations experience came from a time early in her career when she was forced to confront a diagnosis of Lyme Disease while trying to remain engaged and productive at work.

Disclo supports some 30,000 workers with job accommodations at companies worldwide. Customers include established firms as large as Samsung and Kraft Heinz and growing companies such as Webflow, a website development platform.

According to Olson, "We wanted to build an enterprise-ready platform but also catered to the needs of the end user – that being those with disabilities. Our goal was to build a digital platform that simplifies the accommodations process, ensures privacy for employees, and gives companies the tools they need to mitigate legal risk."

Olson provides a beneficial and practical definition of workplace accommodation: "A workplace accommodation is any change to the work environment or job process that helps an employee with a disability perform their job effectively. This could be anything from flexible work schedules to assistive technology. For employees, accommodations ensure they can thrive without sacrificing their well-being."

As we have covered throughout this chapter, asking for workplace accommodation can be very uncomfortable for persons with disabilities. In many cases, employees feel like there are only so many times they can advocate for themselves in the office – be it seeking a raise or promotion or asking to be put on an interesting new project. Suppose someone is already paid less than their co-workers, is facing distance bias, or has a boss unwilling to understand their disability. In that case, the last thing many disabled people want to do is ask for a reasonable accommodation.

With the changes in how people work and the experience of COVID-19, which showed that nearly all of us need reasonable accommodations to do our job, more people than ever are asking for accommodations. "Back in the day, every once in a while, someone would raise their hand and say, 'I need an accommodation.' Because those requests were so infrequent, it wasn't that difficult for a company to manage the process manually," noted Olson.

That way of requesting accommodations was messy and benefitted no one, most certainly the person placing the request. According to Olson, "The old way of handling accommodations—where employees speak directly to a supervisor—often results in inconsistent outcomes and leaves companies vulnerable to legal risk. It also puts undue pressure on employees to disclose sensitive information without guarantees of confidentiality."

Enter Disclo. Its software platform allows employees to confidentially submit accommodation requests without disclosing their disability directly to their employer. It also serves as an independent, third-party verifier of a person's disability.

To help manage the accommodation requests, Disclo creates a customized dashboard for each client to track all related workflows.

Image 4: Disclo Dashboard

Disclosures	GOAL: 7% ⓘ	Requests	GOAL: Not set ⓘ	Case Decision	GOAL: 90% ⓘ
10%	✓	25%		84% Approved	6% Denied
TOTAL EMPLOYEES:	722	TOTAL SIGN-UPS:	253	AVG. TIME TO DECISION	32 Days
TOTAL DISCLOSURES:	72 (10%)	TOTAL REQUESTS:	63 (25%)	TOTAL CASES DECIDED:	57 (90%)

QUICK ACTIONS:

Edit Goals | Invite team members

Image Description: Three columns of data measures across Disclosures, Requests, and Case Decisions. Image provided by Hannah Olson.

When employees submit a workplace accommodation request, Disclo digitally verifies medical records with providers directly in the platform. To ensure accuracy, Disclo keeps Americans with Disabilities Act and Pregnant Workers Fairness Act (PWFA) experts on retainer for any edge cases that may arise with providers, case managers, or employees.

Cases are managed directly in Disclo's Health Insurance Portability and Accountability Act (HIPAA)-compliant platform—from request to decision (including notes and status updates). Disclo also provides time stamps for all communications in the platform and secure documentation for legal defensibility.

Companies benefit from timely, consistent, error-free accommodation decisions that enhance compliance and employee satisfaction. They can also gain insights and trends from the request case history, improving their employee self-ID and accommodation process.

While Disclo provides a variety of benefits such as easing administrative burdens and simplifying the accommodations process, its most impactful outcome is that it dramatically increases the disclosure rate by the employees of its clients. An average of 15 percent of employees at a given company enrolled in Disclo disclose their disability, a stark difference from the three or four percent disclosure rate typical of organizations across the economy. With more employees disclosing their disability safely and constructively, employers enjoy a more robust culture and a more engaged, innovative workforce.

Disclo's future is bright and always innovative. It has raised $6.5 million from venture firms such as Bain Capital Ventures and Y Combinator and continues expanding its offerings. Yet, Hannah Olson and the team never lose focus on what is most important, "At the end of the day, there's a human component to this. Our goal is to marry compliance and technology - leveraging automation and innovation - with personalized support and service, ensuring we're there for people throughout what can be a challenging and overwhelming process."

CHAPTER 5

The Human Toll of Employment Disparities

The most interesting people you'll find are ones
that don't fit into your average cardboard box.
They'll make what they need,
they'll make their own boxes.
—Dr. Temple Grandin,
a professor at Colorado State University (U.S.) with autism

An unfortunate but overlooked fact about disability is that it often costs more to be disabled than non-disabled. These additional costs compound the employment and economic disparities the population with a disability faces. For example, in the United States, "a household containing an adult with a disability that limits their ability to work requires, on average, 28 percent more income (or an additional $17,690 a year) to obtain the same standard of living as a similar household without a member with a disability."[107]

The same is true in Europe, where studies found that disabled people in Sweden pay approximately 22,500€ (about $24,000) annually in additional costs and those in the U.K. pay about 18,000€ (about $19,000) extra a year. That is the ultimate "double whammy" for a person with a disability – their earning potential is frequently limited, yet their basic costs of living can be higher than those of a non-disabled person.

Asia is no different. According to the Asian Development Bank, "Many social protection programs aimed at guaranteeing minimum income do not consider the additional costs of disability when calculating eligibility.

Persons with disabilities are often excluded [from the social programs], even though they face higher risk of living below the established poverty thresholds."[108]

Some of the most severe disparities exist in Latin America and the Caribbean. The World Bank found that stigmatization of disabled people is widespread throughout the region, starting in the educational systems of most countries and continuing through the professional environment. Further, the public policy realm is not empowered to drive change.

Most troubling – 18 countries in Latin America and the Caribbean deny persons with disabilities the right to run for public office. Although "20 countries have created specialized national committees to work on the inclusion of persons with disabilities ... [many] the lack of personnel and resources, and these committees' limited capacity for taking decisions means that they cannot do much to make meaningful changes."[109] Without an empowered public sector, there is little hope for fundamental changes that will dramatically improve employment outcomes among the population of disabled people, let alone enable entrepreneurs to embark upon a career of innovation.

A final reality is that many of us "mask" our true selves by covering up traits that define us as humans in our places of employment. And masking creates stress that has real consequences for individuals and organizations. For example, Deloitte and the Meltzer Center for Diversity, Inclusion, and Belonging at the New York University School of Law recently published a research paper, "Uncovering culture: A call to action for leaders." The research was based on a survey of 1,269 U.S. workers across all industries.

Characterizing the results as "sobering," the authors found that:

- 60 percent of all workers reported covering at work in the last 12 months

- 70 percent of disabled workers covered at work in the previous 12 months

- 68 percent of nonbinary and/or transgender workers covered at work in the last 12 months

- 66 percent of Asian, 65 percent Black, 62 percent Hispanic/ Latin(x/a/e/o), and 56 percent of White workers covered at work[110]

Consider some of the quotes from surveyed individuals:

- "I bury a lot of my emotions and act happy so that coworkers are not reminded of my depression."

- "Since I'm older in IT, I rarely bring up that I'm 62 and near retirement. I don't want to end up laid off because of ageism."

- "I don't want people to know I was poor growing up, so I try not to talk about my childhood at work."[111]

These quotes address a loss of individual freedom or a person's fear of losing it. What these people are essentially saying is, "I don't feel comfortable expressing myself because I know something bad will happen to me if I do." This lack of freedom (either real or perceived) results from most employers' authoritative attitude toward their employees.

In her research about the role of the private sector in society, Princeton University professor Elizabeth Anderson pointedly noted, "Employer authority over workers' off-duty lives is implicit, a byproduct of the employment-at-will rule: since employers may fire workers for any or no reason, they may fire them for their sexual activities, partner choice, or any other choice workers think of as private from their employer, unless the state has enacted a law specifically forbidding employer discrimination on these grounds. Workplace authoritarianism is still with us."[112]

Beyond the impacts on a personal level, the performance of organizations also suffers. Organizations underperform because their people are suffering. The Deloitte and Meltzer Center report concluded, "The costs of covering extend beyond the individual, preventing the organization from realizing the gains that a culture of authenticity and belonging provides. These include reduced turnover risk and employee absenteeism; increased job and team performance, innovation, and engagement; and higher profits when teams are more engaged."[113]

Bringing together the findings from the Deloitte and Meltzer Center study and Professor Anderson's statement that the lives of most workers are dictated by their employers, every organization must take a long, hard look at its culture and policies. A company can have the world's most diverse and talented workforce, but if its workforce does not feel comfortable and empowered, its innovative potential will be lost.

The Consequences of Sidelining Persons with Disabilities

The fact that tens of millions of persons with disabilities around the world are either unemployed or underemployed has consequences far beyond socio-economic statistics. There is an essential human element to structural employment challenges facing the population with disabilities. We live in a society that places intrinsic value on a person's profession and ability to earn an income. Our identity is tied to how we earn a living. As Vilissa Thompson, co-director of the Disability Economic Justice Collaborative at The Century Foundation, noted in testimony before the United States House of Representatives, "Disability can be a factor in whether a person thrives in a country where productivity and one's ability to contribute to the labor force are prioritized more than who they are as an individual and the value they possess that goes beyond their labor to further the economic strength of society."[114]

A significant influence in the struggles of personal and professional identity faced by many disabled people is the perpetual nature of economic insecurity caused by their marginal place in society. When job prospects are dim, discrimination by employers is common, earnings potential is stifled, and the pink slip could be given at any time, a person's feelings of self-worth will suffer. That insecurity has a ripple effect that reaches every part of life – access to housing, healthcare and childcare, healthy food, and reliable transportation. Not to mention the lack of opportunity to take a relaxing vacation or spend quality time with friends and family. When living paycheck to paycheck and feeling marginalized, those moments of joy are few and far between.

A research paper by The Century Foundation declared that economic security is the most pressing challenge facing the disabled population in the United States. "In 1990, [the Americans with Disabilities Act], which today remains the cornerstone of disability civil rights law in the United States, established four goals for disabled Americans: equal opportunity, independent living, full participation, and economic self-sufficiency. Despite three decades of progress, economic security has been the most difficult of the ADA's goals for the United States to realize. It remains out of reach for an unconscionable share of America's disability community."[115]

Adding to the human cost of disability is that accessing social safety net programs – often the only economic lifeline available to persons with disabilities – can be dehumanizing. No matter the country or local jurisdiction, accessing public support, be it income assistance, affordable housing, or job training, requires interaction with the so-called "Administrative State." The Administrative State combines government policies and the public officials tasked with overseeing those policies and implementing them daily.

It is not the intent of *Case Studies in Disability Driven Innovation* to question the merits of laws and regulatory policies to safeguard the rights of individuals with disabilities. After all, I worked for United States Senator Tom Harkin, the lead Senate sponsor of the Americans with Disabilities Act, who was also instrumental in enacting many other legislative measures that protect the rights of persons with disabilities and foster competitive, integrated employment in the workplace. Nor is it the intent of this book to vilify the public sector officials at all levels of government tasked with implementing public policy or helping persons with disabilities and their families navigate the various programs designed to improve their quality of life.

However, The Center for American Progress made clear that the reality is that too many so-called "safety net" programs have a high cost on the disabled population. Notably, "For disabled people in America, barriers to critical, lifesaving safety net programs are too often a part of everyday life. These barriers, known as 'administrative burdens,' are roughly defined as any challenge that makes it difficult for someone to access or maintain assistance for which they otherwise qualify."[116] In the same report, The Center for American Progress identified a range of barriers, "including lengthy and complicated paperwork, asset tests, inflexible in-person appointments, backlogs with long wait times, inaccessible and poorly designed websites, and complex and confusing application processes."[117]

The Center for American Progress research further asserted, "Administrative burdens cause real, lasting harm to huge swaths of disabled Americans, making it difficult for them to navigate a system that is supposed to help them cover basic necessities such as food, housing, and medical treatments."[118]

"Stacking"

Stacking is a term I use to refer to the interconnected challenges that persons with disabilities face every day. Many – but certainly not all – disabled people do not believe their disability impedes their life or careers. Instead, it is an advantage that allows them to have a different perspective on all their experiences. But what is universal across the disabled population is that society's barriers and norms are often stifling and add extreme stress and hardship to their lives.

Rather than always treating the disability as a condition to be managed, it is more important to consider the ecosystem in which that person operates – the mindset of the Social Model of disability covered in Chapter 4. A person with a mobility limitation may be perfectly comfortable with their disability. What causes them stress is knowing they need to be at an important meeting at a specific time but to get there, they must first manage an unreliable community transit network or the lack of accessibility in the neighborhood subway station. Someone else may be worried about their daycare provider increasing the cost of care, which would impact their careers.

Anyone invested in the success of a person with a disability – whether a supervisor, a friend, a mentor, or an investor – must understand the entire environment in which they operate. We no longer have the luxury of separating work from home and vice versa. If we want people to bring their best selves to an innovative project, we must create a forum where that can happen.

Hannah Bouline stressed the importance of providing "wraparound services" to all employees to drive innovation and growth:

Some people have had throughout their lives great access to an understanding of the disability, benefit system, and world because they had very strong parent advocates. They had case managers. Other people we come across or are referred to us or come to us have never had any of that. Maybe they don't have a diagnosis. Maybe they don't have a case manager.

That doesn't mean that we, as a business, necessarily have to provide all of those things directly. But it does mean we're tapped into this world. We want to make sure that everyone has those things in place that they need to be successful.

"Sometimes that can be using our connections to engage benefit systems or vocational rehab managers. Other times it's asking baseline questions like, 'Do you have a bank account?' or 'What's your tech literacy level?' Having answers to those questions allows us to set people up for greater success in their jobs and their personal wellness.

Barriers to the Earning and Entrepreneurship Potential of Persons with Disabilities

The most consequential barriers are those public policies and laws limiting the disabled population's earnings and savings potential. Disability-driven innovation is, at its core, entrepreneurship. Entrepreneurs must be fairly compensated for bringing their ideas to market, regardless of their disability status. While every entrepreneur and innovator invariably faces myriads of challenges, those with disabilities face widespread discrimination that is often entrenched in decades-old government policies.

Many countries have established programs like the Social Security benefits that are in place in the United States. Specific to the United States, the Social Security Administration administers two programs that provide disability benefits. The first is the Social Security disability insurance (SSDI) which provides insurance to persons with disabilities who have paid into the Social Security Trust Fund but, due to their disability, cannot work at a level of substantial gainful activity (SGA). The second program is Supplemental Security Income (SSI), a needs-based benefit to low-income individuals with disabilities paid out by the pre-established Federal benefit rate. Unlike the SSDI program, funded through workers' payroll contributions, the SSI program is paid out of the U.S. Treasury General Fund (like most government programs). SSI benefits pay for basic human needs such as food, medicine, clothing, and shelter. Through these initiatives, people who qualify for SSI either have no income or have a meager income due to their disability and receive a regular (usually monthly) financial payment as a form of "safety net."

Despite the good intentions, there are three common shortcomings with these financial assistance programs:

1. At best, the monthly benefit payment is just enough to keep persons with disabilities at or above the poverty line. In most cases, the monthly benefits barely cover basic living expenses and nothing more, including more substantial health care treatments or transportation needs.

2. The application process to qualify for these benefits can be complex, invasive, and time-consuming, often requiring access to computers connected to the Internet or transportation to the program's administrative staff's office.

3. The legal complexity around the disability benefits system is unnecessarily complex and the fear of incorrectly following the guidelines often serves as a powerful disincentive for persons with disabilities to be employed or launch a business.

The income limits for many disability benefits are a particular burden on persons with disabilities and, ultimately, a drag on the global economy's performance. In the United States, the amount of SSDI assistance a person can receive is not established by a set income threshold per se. Instead, it is through what the Social Security Administration (SSA) defines as "substantial gainful activity." In 2023, the SGA amount is $1,470 in gross wages for disabled applicants and $2,460 in gross wages for blind applicants. Suppose a person earns more than those thresholds. In that case, they are not considered disabled (per the SSA definition) because they are engaging in substantial gainful activity, and their benefits are terminated (although they can be reinstated if the earned income falls below the $1,470 and $2,460 monthly thresholds).[119] Because of the threshold limits, there is a pronounced disincentive for many persons with disabilities to enter the workforce.

Compounding the problem with SSI benefits are the equally strict limits on the ability of persons with disabilities and their families to build adequate savings, such as cash reserves, stocks, and mutual fund holdings. According to Kathleen Romig and colleagues and the Center on Budget and Policy Priorities, "Eligibility is limited to people who have only $2,000 (or $3,000 for couples). This is not enough for beneficiaries to weather an emergency, let alone provide stability or save for the future. Administering the resource limit often referred to as an asset test, is burdensome for both Social Security Administration staff and claimants."[120]

Like the income limits, having personal savings more than the thresholds could lead to suspension from the SSI program. As a result, the personal savings threshold often serves as a disincentive for disabled people to engage in entrepreneurship and other economic activities. To its credit, SSA does have in place work incentives that are intended to encourage people to obtain employment. However, navigating the SSA is so complex and challenging that those incentives can be easily overlooked or misunderstood.

Medicaid is another important U.S. government program designed to provide necessary healthcare services to persons with disabilities. The intent behind the Medicaid support of these services is correct – helping people maintain their health so they participate in the workforce and ideally enjoy a higher quality of life. For example, Medicaid can provide services such as:

- Personal care
- Assistive technologies (devices such as wheelchairs, hearing aids, or screen readers)
- Supported living (such as help finding and maintaining housing)
- Supported employment (such as help finding and maintaining employment)
- Transportation

The income limits to qualify for a waiver that allows persons with disabilities to access Medicaid services vary but are based on inputs such as the poverty level established by the U.S. government, the type of disability, age, family status, and access to caregivers. A few states have either eliminated income limits or are considering doing so, which has a potentially positive outcome for persons with disabilities but also adds to the complexity surrounding service eligibility. Further, applying for and maintaining the waiver is extraordinarily complex and time-consuming, often requiring medical documentation, physician testimonials, and detailed health records.

The complexity of the income limits impacts other government initiatives designed to increase the household income of low and moderate-wage earners. The United States has long had the Earned Income Credit (EIC) in place, which allows approximately 25 million low and moderate workers to offset a significant portion of their federal taxes or, in some cases, receive a cash credit for taxes paid. Yet, disabled people face substantial challenges in determining eligibility for the EIC, what types of income (including assistance payments such as SSI), and what amounts of disability insurance are treated as income. It is no wonder that about 20 percent of all taxpayers eligible for the EIC do not bother applying for it.

Compounding the complexities of national-level policies in the United States is the patchwork of policies in the 50 states. Among many states, there are different approaches for fostering employment, often contradictory eligibility requirements for public assistance, and intractable bureaucracies. Sara Hart Weir, the Executive Director of the Kansas Council on Developmental Disabilities, provides one example of the challenges:

> *Think about a military family that moves from state to state every couple of years. That family is caregiving for a child with a disability. Think about all the things they need to deal with to find employment for the child after each move. For example, how do we ensure that when they move from North Carolina to Kansas they don't go to the end of the list for things like a Home and Community-Based Waiver to be eligible for certain health care supports for the child? Or do they need to go through another assessment process to identify what jobs are best for the child even though the child already has a track record of employment?[121]*

These outdated and unproductive policies are not limited to the United States. Across Europe, there is a patchwork of "quota systems, wage subsidies, tax reductions for companies employing persons with disabilities, assistance for training costs and

reasonable accommodation ... and the possibility to retain certain disability benefits while in work."[122] According to an analysis of 35 European countries conducted by Isabel Baptista and Eric Marlier for the European Commission, the challenges to people with disabilities in Europe are on par with those in the U.S. For example, the process to claim a disability is lengthy, income support for the population is inadequate, and the income thresholds can be a disincentive to employment and entrepreneurship.[123]

Although data from Asia is less comprehensive than that of the United States and Europe, the Asian Development Bank has noted that the disabled population in Asia faces the same barriers. Notably, "the entry into employment of persons with disabilities is disincentivized since disability-specific benefits are means-tested and can be taken away if income increases."[124]

Consider the following statement from James Warnken, a digital accessibility specialist, entrepreneur, and consultant about how the current policies treat him: "It just kind of traps you in this ecosystem where the more money you make, the more money you lose from that government program. There's so much extra effort that, as a person with a disability, we are expected to do to be independent and successful. It is not even close to a level playing field."[125]

Section 14(c): The Worst of the Worst

The most counterproductive – and by far the most demeaning – policy in the United States is the so-called "sub-minimum wage." In 1938, Congress passed the Fair Labor Standards Act (FLSA). Section 14(c) of the law "authorizes employers, after receiving a certificate from the Wage and Hour Division, to pay subminimum wages – wages less than the Federal minimum wage – to workers who have disabilities for the work being performed. Even worse, the workers compensated under Section 14(c) are often placed in a separate work environment than their non-disabled counterparts. In other words, the U.S. government has had a policy in place since 1938 that allows employers to actively discriminate against not just the earnings potential of employees with disabilities but also their status in places of employment.

According to the U.S. Government Accountability Office, it is estimated there are about 1,200 employers in the United States who hold Section 14(c) certificates, thereby allowing them to pay qualifying employees a sub-minimum wage. A 2020 report by the U.S. Commission on Civil

Rights conservatively approximates that more than 100,000 people are employed under the 14(c) framework, with an average wage of $3.34 per hour – less than half of the hourly federal minimum wage of $7.25.[126] As a point of context, a $3.34 hourly wage means the average person with a disability who is employed under 14(c) earned "just $53.44 per week or $213.76 per month."[127]

As if the wage disparities are not bad enough, an investigation by the *Washington Post* found that, between 2010 and 2022, organizations holding 14(c) certificates "racked up" over $20 million in unpaid back wages to their employees.[128] To be crystal clear on this point – a significant number of 14(c) organizations can't be bothered to pay their employees ANY wage, let alone one that is well below minimum wage.

Image 5: Back wages owed by employers holding 14(c) certificates to their workers[129]

14(c) employers rack up over $20M in back wages owed to workers

Back wages assessed by the Department of Labor for all 14(c) violations by employers for each year between 2010 and 2022

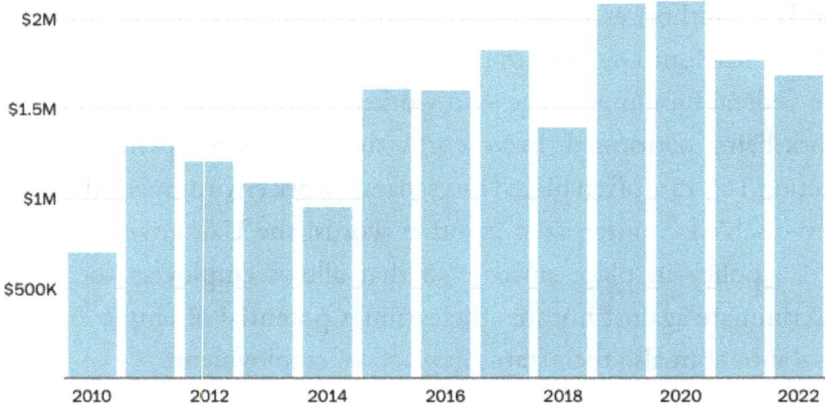

Image Description: A bar chart representing the amounts of back wages owed by employers to workers classified under 14(c) from 2010 to 2022. Source: Washington Post.

As Image 5 indicates, the general delinquency trend shows a higher dollar amount of unpaid wages in the later years of the study than in the earlier years. The problem is getting worse, not better.

In November 2024, Keely Cat-Wells, an entrepreneur, disability rights advocate, and co-founder of technology and media company Making Space published a powerful essay in *Time* magazine about the inherent flaws of 14(c). Perhaps the most serious flaw of 14(c) is that it perpetuates discrimination against persons with disabilities for the advantage of others. As Cat-Wells wrote about 14(c), "It has become a convenient loophole for employers to secure cheap labor while exploiting disabled workers without facing any consequences. By allowing these practices to continue, we are enabling the exploitation of an already marginalized group, further entrenching them in poverty rather than providing opportunities for growth and independence."

Factors Behind Flawed Public Policies

Arguably, the primary reason for the many shortcomings of public policy is they embody the medical mindset to disability. The demeaning mindset asserts it is the person's disability that prevents them from being employed.

Yes, it is true that, in some cases, persons with disabilities (or any of us) cannot work or choose not to be part of the workforce. The reality is that most disabled people can work and want to be in the workforce, either as employees or entrepreneurs. Society's barriers prevent them from fully participating in the workforce. For those people, many public policies are a powerful disincentive to maximizing their career and earning potential.

Another powerful disincentive is loss aversion. People are worried about losing their benefits, including access to health care. Out of fear, many proactively decide to self-limit their employment and career potential.

The complexity of the administrative systems compounds this mindset. It is only natural for a person to think, "It was so hard to get my SSI payments and Medicaid set up. I need those payments to cover my rent and food. So, I am not doing anything that will jeopardize my SSI money and my healthcare through Medicaid."

Another reason for the policy shortcomings is an obsolete mentality that is so overly focused on providing a minimum level of social and financial support that earnings and entrepreneurial potential are ignored. The policies wrongly assume disabled people are not – and cannot be – powerful economic contributors. As *Case Studies in Disability Driven Innovation* will demonstrate time and time again, the market – and thus the value to be created – for disability-centric products and services is global in scale and worth trillions of dollars. That market will only grow over time.

Building on that point, many public policies also need to account for the value-creating potential of disabled-led businesses and their employees. Treating disability inclusion as a compliance requirement diminishes its innovative and profit-generating potential. Compliance with the law is merely the foundation of what is needed for disability employment. Without question, a good foundation of public policy is necessary. But foundations are static, designed to support rather than grow and evolve. Similarly, disability inclusion policies too often fail to be forward-looking. Nor do they do a great job appreciating that innovation represents the future potential of disability employment.

In linking civil rights, employment, innovation, and entrepreneurship, Regina Kline astutely remarked, "The public systems that are in place are there to protect individuals from harm from exploitation, to safeguard civil rights. The great promise of civil rights is to safeguard people's right to participate in society. And part of that is full participation in the economy. And so there is unfinished business from a civil rights perspective to make sure that people with disabilities are not just included in the workforce but also able to fully participate in the innovation economy."[130]

Finally, the reality is that many public policies are simply outdated. Not only are the policies overly burdensome on the disabled population, but they also need to reflect today's reality. For example, the SSDI program and Supplemental Security Income (SSI) were implemented in the United States decades before the ADA was signed into law. The SSDI and SSI programs assume that most disabled people cannot – and never will – have anything approaching a career. Yet, a key pillar of the ADA is creating competitive, integrated employment for persons with disabilities. The success of one of the world's major civil rights measures is held back by the antiquated policies of other laws – a classic Catch-22.[131]

There is no benefit to anyone that comes from disincentivizing people from working. It just compounds the reality that persons with disabilities are penalized and marginalized for reasons entirely out of their control.

The human toll of disability goes beyond flaws in public policy or a person's interactions with their employer or the public sector. For many, the simple desire to meet at a friend's house is a challenge unless that house is accessible and has universal design features—things most residences do not have. The lack of accessibility only reinforces the sense of isolation borne by countless disabled people.

Case Study: Vertical Harvest: A Model of Competitive, Integrated Employment

Headquartered in Jackson, Wyoming (U.S.), Vertical Harvest is a farming company that grows its crops indoors and vertically rather than the traditional method of horizontal growing in open fields. Its business model is built on working "with communities to develop underutilized space in urban, underserved neighborhoods, grow 'up' on a fraction of the land required by traditional agriculture, while using 85 percent less water to deliver our produce at peak flavor and nutrition, year-round."

Beyond being an innovator in the agricultural sector, Vertical Harvest is unique because it was founded on the premise of competitive, integrated employment. Caroline Croft Estay is Vertical Harvest's Co-Founder and Chief Potential Officer. After moving to Jackson, she started her career working with students who have disabilities in the community's school system. In 2016, she and Nona Yehia embarked upon a journey to create North America's first hydroponic greenhouse (a greenhouse where plants are not grown in soil but rather in a water-based nutrient solution, rather than in soil, in an artificial environment).

From her work in Jackson's schools, Caroline knew that many youth and young professionals in the community had – at best – limited job and career prospects. Yet, local employers often have trouble finding employees. Croft Estay said, "Hey, I'm a case manager and a provider for the more than four percent of our population in Jackson who identify with a disability. And they've got no future work. Because I knew so many of the people in the community, I was able to champion them and bring them into our company."

"Within those first few years, it was all hands on deck. Not only did we have to learn to grow, but we literally had to learn one another. I came to the job knowing somebody who identifies as autistic. They do better with the sequential order of the day and task list. That mindset helped us. We got through each day by doing this task, then this task, and so on."

As she helped build the company's operational side, Croft Estay also developed Grow Well – Vertical Harvest's cultural framework. Grow Well is Vertical Harvest's "...customized employment model that fosters professional development, personal discovery, and community impact. Our person-centered approach aligns professional, personal, and community components of the workplace, ensuring the development of job skills, self-growth, accountability, and engaged citizenship. The model is designed to foster and facilitate a culture of inclusion and equity."

Its customized employment approach seeks to match a person's skills with jobs while appreciating that skills and interests evolve. A person's starting job may not be their career destination. "The customized employment approach requires us to ask questions like, 'What does the business need? Are you going to be in the microgreen department? Are you better at packaging? Are you maybe going to be best served in the retail space?' This is about being a human-centered business and looking at every one of us as human beings," said Croft Estay. "We ask everyone, 'What is your human potential?' Yes, we are here to run a business. We need to make a profit. But we can only do that when everyone is in the right place doing what is best for themselves and the business."

In speaking with some employees of Vertical Harvest, it is clear that the core element of the Grow Well model and, by extension, customized employment is the necessity for constant and ongoing communication between everyone in the company. The open lines of communication apply to the daily responsibilities of running a company and ensuring that the employees bring their best selves to work daily. As Sean Stone, the Facilities Lead, who has an intellectual disability said, "I like how we start every day. The first thing I do is talk to my boss and figure out the plan for the day and the timeline. It helps me to know what needs to get done."

Amanda MacFarlane, who has moved from the marketing department to packaging and now is the assistant to the CEO, talked about the ongoing opportunities to engage with her manager about her career interests. "By speaking up I was able to go further in my career," noted Amanda. "Plus, with the injuries to my feet, I can't stand up all day. So, we worked together to come up with a solution that helps me and the company."

Regular communications have also normalized the accommodation process. Amanda could move to a job that allowed her to sit rather than stand. Nikki Thompson, a Grow Well Associate, talked about how she does "90 percent of my job from home and on my own time. They trust me to do my job and get it done right."

Vertical Harvest's customized employment model requires everyone to be fully vested in it – every hour of every day. As McFarlane stated, "There is a lot of responsibility on us. We have to communicate with everyone. We recently had an Upskilling Training, and we learned how to communicate better, not just with managers but with each other. We were told not to assume anything. We have to talk to each other. Communication is the key to every relationship here."

It is also important to remember that there are no days off in farming. "The plants don't stop growing on the weekend," stated Croft Estay. "It's labor intensive. We are trying to pair technology and automation with the needed skills. Which means we need to take a people-first approach to the business."

The most exciting thing about Vertical Harvest is that its future is growing – pun intended! It is soon opening a new, larger vertical farming facility in Maine. As in Wyoming, a revolutionary approach to farming is paired with a transformative approach to employment. The communities of Maine and beyond are certain to benefit.

Where Do We Go From Here?

As we will cover in the next chapter, powerful transformations are underway in how we work to drive lasting change to disability employment. Those come with promise and peril. They are breaking down barriers across all sectors of the economy, changing the concept of "work," and allowing for greater flexibility in how we collaborate. They likely will force policymakers to improve the foundation of disability employment. Yet, there is a real risk that those transformations push many people closer to the economy's margins and could be barriers to nourishing career growth.

One positive is that some countries appear to be in the early stages of evolving their policies to better reflect the intersectional nature of disability and the changing nature of employment. According to research by the International Labour Organization (ILO) Organization for Economic Co-operation and Development (OECD) of several countries around the world, "Policy objectives are now shifting in these countries towards the search for a new balance between two simultaneous goals: i) to provide an adequate and secure income for those who cannot work and their families; while ii) providing good incentives and supports to work for those who can."

We must recognize that we do not need to wait for public policy changes to foster equitable compensation practices for persons with disabilities – not just in pay but also in benefits packages and workplace accommodations. Policy complexities aside, there is nothing legally stopping employers (be they in the public, private, or non-profit sectors) from paying workers with disabilities a livable wage and providing them with the same benefits as non-disabled workers.

In the United States, companies such as Voya Financial, Microsoft, and JPMorgan Chase are partnering with a plethora of organizations such as the Office Disability Employment Policy at the U.S. Department of Labor, Council of State Administrators of Vocational Rehabilitation, American Association of People with Disabilities, CEO Commission on Disability Employment, and the National Down Syndrome Society (NDSS) to push for several policy measures that will address pressing issues, such as eliminating Section 14(c), raising the income limits for SSDI assistance, and allowing people to better save for their retirement.

Despite the active support of those leaders, the reality is there are organizations, policymakers, and companies committed to maintaining policies such as 14(c) because it is in their economic self-interest. The misguided and outdated laws need to be changed to reflect the realities of today's economy and the lives of persons with disabilities.

The only way that will happen is if there is greater engagement and representation of persons with disabilities in the political system. That representation must occur at all levels. As Sara Hart Weir stated, "We need people to be in places where we are currently not. More representation is needed in Congress and in state legislatures, and even at the local level in our communities."[132]

CHAPTER 6

The Disruptions to Employment and Innovation

When the paradigm shifts, do you have something to contribute? Because there is no God-given right to exist if you don't have anything relevant.
—Sataya Nadella, CEO, Microsoft

Since 2020, five transformations have fundamentally – and permanently – changed the way we collaborate and innovate. The new paradigm has opportunities and risks, especially for persons with disabilities. The first transformation is the COVID-19 pandemic that ran rampant in early 2020 and remains with us today. The early months of the pandemic unleashed a technology-based way of working that suddenly changed how large segments of the workforce do their jobs. People now use technology to overcome time and distance, and the expectation of in-person work is declining – a situation familiar to many persons with disabilities.

Second, the concept of "team" within organizations is evolving. Gone is the management approach where homogenous teams operated on distinct projects in a siloed manner, often removed from the organization – the so-called "skunk works." Instead, the most effective teams are designed to be intersectional across organizations, drawing from different points of view and skill sets. The mindset of new approaches to team structures is built around a mindset of collaboration and inclusion to drive innovation.

Third, culture is becoming essential for organizations to sustain brand and reputational strength over time. This trend embodies the abiding leadership mindset: "You are only as good as your people." A strong culture is the antithesis of compliance, mind-numbing rules, and micromanagement by leaders and managers. It allows employees to think outside the box, try new ideas, and find better solutions.

Fourth, the emergence of powerful artificial intelligence (AI) technologies could be the most consequential disruptor of our future. All of us – regardless of disability – face the reality that AI will disrupt our personal and professional lives for the foreseeable future. There is no getting around that fact. The consensus is that AI does pose risks and challenges to employees with disabilities in the workforce. Yet AI "has the potential to create more inclusive and accommodating environments," and it can help remove systemic barriers to competitive, integrated employment."[133] Conceivably, the most exciting and potentially transformative opportunity AI presents to persons with disabilities is its ability to scale innovation and more quickly turn ideas into viable products and services.

A fifth, and arguably the most problematic transformation, is the workplace politicization of culture and values. This transformation has no apparent upside. Instead, it has made professional environments more complicated, stressful, and contentious for everyone, especially those on the organization's fringes or who do not fit the stereotypical definition of a "traditional employee." There is no easy solution on the horizon of this transformation, and there is little chance that the politicization of culture and values will soon diminish.

Despite these transformations (and the promise held in most of them), significant barriers remain to creating truly inclusive, equitable workplaces that allow us to bring our best selves to work. Notably, the need for more appreciation of what constitutes a reasonable accommodation in the workplace and the inconsistent application of universal design practices across every part of our lives must be overcome to maximize our innovative potential.

These disruptions apply to all organizations across society, from legacy companies to startups in their infancy. Startups' newness gives them an advantage in becoming more resilient to these disruptions compared to established organizations. The fresher and smaller a venture is, the more evergreen it is. Early stages of maturity allow organizations to be more adaptable and open to instilling necessary cultural competencies like an organizational appreciation for diverse talents and a mindset that reasonable accommodations benefit all employees.

Transformation #1: COVID-19 and Its Aftermath

The events of March 2020 dramatically revealed that the technology-driven approach to work that persons with disabilities had frequently used to engage in their careers was the reasonable accommodation most of us needed in a crisis. Further, the disruptions of the pandemic altered the nature of employment across the global economy. The traditional 9-5 job is gone, the 5-day work week enshrined in the early 1900s is becoming a 4-day work week, and the bonds between employers and employees are frayed.

The early days of the COVID-19 pandemic were a stark reminder to workers that no one's job was safe. The Great Resignation following the pandemic was an equally stark reminder to employers that their employees no longer felt a deep loyalty to their bosses.

While those changes impact us all, arguably, the disabled population will most acutely feel the effects. There are wildly differing opinions on the pros and cons of the upheaval caused by the pandemic and the subsequent transition to remote work. On one hand, the early days of the pandemic showed that technology platforms such as Zoom, Teams, and Slack could effectively span time and location while allowing people to connect with friends, families, and colleagues. All of us were living, working, and engaging with people from all over the world in the same manner that persons with disabilities had done for generations.

Yet, the dangers of remote and flexible work are especially acute for employees with disabilities and other marginalized populations. In November 2020, Lisa Schur and colleagues at the U.S.-based National Library of Medicine noted, "Potential downsides for all workers include greater social isolation, increasingly blurred lines between work and home life, and being "out of sight, out of mind" for promotion and training opportunities. All these drawbacks may particularly impact more marginalized groups such as people with disabilities, women, people of color, and the LGBTQ community."[134]

A September 2020 *New York Times* article by Nelson Schwartz covered many challenges marginalized employees face in a remote work environment. In the article, Schwartz interviewed Evelyn Carter, a managing director at Paradigm, a consulting firm, who raised the concept of "distance bias." According to Carter, distance bias is when "You put more emphasis on people closer to you. You don't have connections where you don't have proximity, so you maintain relationships with the people you already know."[135]

Distance bias can be costly. As Joy Fitzgerald, the chief diversity and inclusion officer at Eli Lilly, observed, "To succeed, 50 percent is performance, 25 percent is perception, and the other 25 percent, which is a force multiplier, is visibility. But if people don't know you, they don't see you. It creates a higher degree of complexity and challenge for underrepresented groups."[136]

These observations convey that more things have stayed the same for all that has changed with a sharp rise in remote, technology-driven work environments. The extra convenience is welcomed, but if getting to the office regularly is challenging, you risk being forgotten or passed over by colleagues. The institutional behaviors and biases leading to distance bias in organizations are not necessarily intentional, but the outcome is the same.

Persons with disabilities face another significant challenge in achieving recognition in the workplace – their loyalty is often taken for granted. Managers usually assume that because disabled employees are less likely than their non-disabled counterparts to change jobs, they are inherently loyal. And that misleading narrative has become part of the selling point for hiring persons with disabilities. A basic internet search will reveal any number of articles, research papers, and blog posts touting the loyalty of employees with disabilities. Even respected, peer-reviewed publications cite loyalty and motivation as essential economic reasons to hire persons with disabilities.[137]

Countless employees with disabilities are indeed loyal for all the right reasons. They enjoy their work, appreciate their colleagues, and contribute to the advancement of the organization. However, the reality for many persons with disabilities is far harsher and more complex. Steve Foresti, a senior advisor to Wilshire Associates, a global investment advisory and asset management firm, and someone who has had Stargardt disease since he was seven made clear that many employees with disabilities are loyal because they are stuck in their current roles. The burden of transitioning to a new job should be lowered. "People love the stat about employees with disabilities being so loyal," said Foresti. "The prospect of me going and looking for another job or job hopping and figuring out the commute was a nightmare. The onboarding, the reentry, getting people comfortable, getting myself comfortable, and the environment. The proposition of bouncing around for an extra couple thousand bucks a year was never on my mind."[138]

Steve only alludes to the challenges that come with a person deciding whether to disclose a disability. Again, the reality for many is harsh and complex. Leaving a job that is stable and a known factor in their life is a considerable risk when going to a new job may require that person to disclose their disability.

Despite the growing use of accommodations, remote work, and flexible work schedules by all employees, persons with disabilities still face a high degree of stigma in the workplace. Because of the risks associated with distance bias, the frustrations that come with feeling stuck in a job, or a simple desire to "fit in," millions of people do not disclose their disability in the workplace. An unfortunate reality of the lack of workplace disclosure is that it creates a vicious cycle. As fewer people talk about their connection to disability, there is no incentive for anyone to be open about their connection to disability. As a result, we are not always showing off our best selves and our best talents. That, in turn, limits our ability to achieve a professional culture of openness, acceptance, and innovation across the global economy.

Five years after the onset of the COVID-19 pandemic, the outcome is a mixed bag for persons with disabilities. The broader adoption of remote and technology-based work has further integrated many employees with disabilities into organizations, but not all. Distance bias, barriers to job and career mobility, and the lack of opportunity for people to talk about disability means that too many people remain stuck in outdated and inequitable professional environments. Thus, the promise and excitement in early 2020 driven by the belief that a technology-based workforce will significantly benefit the working population with disabilities has quickly faded. Despite the inconsistent benefits to persons with disabilities, the more significant application of technology into our work environments will continue to accelerate for the foreseeable future.

Ageism in the workforce is another disturbing trend that emerged after the COVID-19 pandemic. While a specific trend is hard to pinpoint at the time of the writing of this book in late 2024, it is becoming clear that more workers over 50 are facing ageism, especially in the United States. Workers in that demographic are much more expensive for companies to keep on the books as compared to younger workers – their salaries are higher, and their benefits cost more to maintain. In previous generations, seniority was considered an insurance policy against layoffs as younger, less tenured employees often bore the brunt of layoffs. That is no longer the case. Not only are older employees at risk of being the first to be laid off, but they are also increasingly the last to be rehired.

The consequences of ageism in the workforce appear to be particularly afflicting older white men. There is a YouTube channel called "TheFadingMan," and its subtitle is "Fading into Oblivion, One Day at a Time." As one reviewer of the channel wrote in a *Medium* post, "I found this channel called TheFadingMan, which features a guy in his mid-50s talking about depression, getting laid off, and other older worker issues. In other videos, TheFadingMan talks about getting the run-around in interviews, job scams, misrepresented job ads, trying to lose weight, getting ghosted by employers, and being broke."[139]

Transformation #2: The Promise and Peril of Artificial Intelligence

Just as the world is moving on from the disruption of the COVID-19 pandemic, artificial intelligence (AI) has emerged as an even more powerful disruptor – for good and bad –impacting every industry in the world. From call centers in the Philippines to shop floors at manufacturing facilities in Mexico to predictive analytics in healthcare, AI advances human-centric outcomes in a way never witnessed in history. Persons with disabilities in the workforce are particularly at risk due to this evolution. As covered in previous chapters, they tend to be in entry-level positions and on the margins of organizational hierarchies. AI is having the most immediate impact on the workforce in these exact areas.

Despite the drawbacks, AI's potential payoff is so enormous that any organization that fails to capitalize on its benefits risks its future. Organizations will only accelerate the pace of AI innovation and adaptation, not slow it down.

Through its far-reaching applications, AI comes in many forms. The integration of Apple's Siri technology into the iOS operating system in 2011 is acknowledged as the first widespread integration of AI into the mass consumer market. Since then, AI has expanded into four main buckets as defined by IBM, the global technology company:

1. Reactive Machine AI. These systems have no memory, work only with currently available data, and are designed to perform particular tasks. One of the first iterations of Reactive Machine AI is IBM's so-called "Deep Blue," which competed in a chess match against grandmaster Gary Kasparov in the late 1990s. Deep Blue could only analyze the pieces on the chess board as they were currently positioned, but it could predict the outcomes of a future move.

2. Limited Memory AI. This form of AI can "use past data for a specific amount of time; it can't retain that data in a library of past experiences to use over a long-term period. As it's trained on more data over time, Limited Memory AI can improve in performance." Limited Memory AI is becoming commonplace through software such as ChatGPT and Grammarly, virtual assistants like Alexa and Siri, and the navigation features of self-driving cars.

3. Theory of Mind AI. Theory of Mind AI is only in the theoretical stages of development. It can "infer human motives and reasoning," and "AI researchers hope it will have the ability to analyze voices, images, and other kinds of data to recognize, simulate, monitor, and respond appropriately to humans on an emotional level. To date, Emotion AI is unable to understand and respond to human feelings."

4. Self-Aware AI. Like Theory of Mind AI, Self-Aware AI is theoretical, and "If ever achieved, it would have the ability to understand its internal conditions and traits along with human emotions and thoughts. It would also have its own set of emotions, needs, and beliefs."[140]

Deloitte's "The State of Generative AI in the Enterprise" report, published in the third quarter of 2024, found that "Two-thirds of organizations are increasing investments after seeing strong value to date. A large percentage (42 percent) report efficiency, productivity, and cost reduction as their single, most important benefit achieved. However, most respondents (58 percent) reported a range of other benefits – highlighting the versatility of GenAI in the enterprise." The other benefits identified by Deloitte include:

- Greater innovation
- Improved products and services
- Enhanced client/customer relationships
- Faster software development
- Increased revenue[141]

The consensus among persons evaluating the promise and pitfalls from the perspective of disability is that AI is a value add, both personally and professionally. "AI-based software can truly be an assistive technology, enabling people to do things they otherwise would be excluded from. AI could give a disabled person agency and autonomy," noted Steven Aquino, a freelance tech journalist who identifies as disabled and writes about accessibility and assistive technologies. For example, Aquino points out that the advancement from the "flip phones" of the 1990s to the larger screen and the AI-powered apps of the Apple iPhone dramatically improved the quality of his life. "For those who, like me, are blind or have low vision, the ability to summon a ride on demand and go anywhere without imposing on anyone else for help is a huge deal."[142]

A recent report by Chloé Touzet of the Organization for Economic Co-operation and Development (OECD) provides more context to the broad array of areas in which AI is adding value to the lives of persons with disabilities. According to Touzet, AI-powered solutions can be classified into four groups:

1. Disability-centered solutions. The most common form of AI solutions focuses on providing workarounds for people with disabilities. Examples of disability-centered solutions include live captioning algorithms or image recognition tools.

2. Environmental adaptation solutions. These solutions allow content and workplaces to be accessible rather than expecting employees with disabilities to be the ones who must adapt. Examples range from AI-powered indoor positioning systems that make physical spaces more accessible to blind and low-vision persons to tools that better match people with job openings.

3. Solutions improving accessibility at a meta-level. This solution applies to broader, often organization-wide, processes and procedures that will enhance accessibility and improve employee efficiency. An example of this is a portal where any employee can request a need for a workplace accommodation.

4. Solutions unlocking new opportunities for people with disability. This is the smallest area of AI innovation and involves using AI to create new job opportunities for job seekers with disabilities that were previously closed to them. An example provided by Touzet is one in which "AI-powered remote operation technologies in logistics and transportation, which can make jobs such as forklift operator accessible to people with physical disabilities."[143]

The biggest challenge for the disability community with AI is ensuring that its constant evolution never becomes inaccessible to people. "The main lesson to be learned from the literature, and our own experiences, is the importance of involving disabled people in the design of AI software and technology which is intended for use by those with disabilities," wrote Peter Smith and Laura Smith in an opinion paper published in *AI and Ethics*. The authors continued, "It is no good waiting until the testing or evaluation stage to involve disabled people. This needs to happen as soon as design begins. What is needed is true co-design, where disabled people are part of the design team and the process of design. This should include a representative group of people with a diverse range of disabilities. Of course, this is not easy to do; however, it is also vital if AI technology is to achieve its true potential."[144]

Because we are in the infancy of AI, the best approach is to treat it as a blank slate. The more people with disabilities engage with AI platforms, the more AI tools can integrate disability's mindset, considerations, and cultural ethos. AI tools are only as good as their inputs – no matter their intended purpose. Perhaps the most overused – but entirely accurate – phrase in the AI conversation is "Garbage in, garbage out." If poor inputs go into AI tools such as Chat GPT, Microsoft Copilot, and Google Gemini, poor answers will come from user queries.

Consider the two queries I submitted to OpenArt, an AI-powered image-generating platform.

Query One: "Create an image of a blind male walking down the street and using a cane."

Image 6: An AI-generated depiction of a blind male

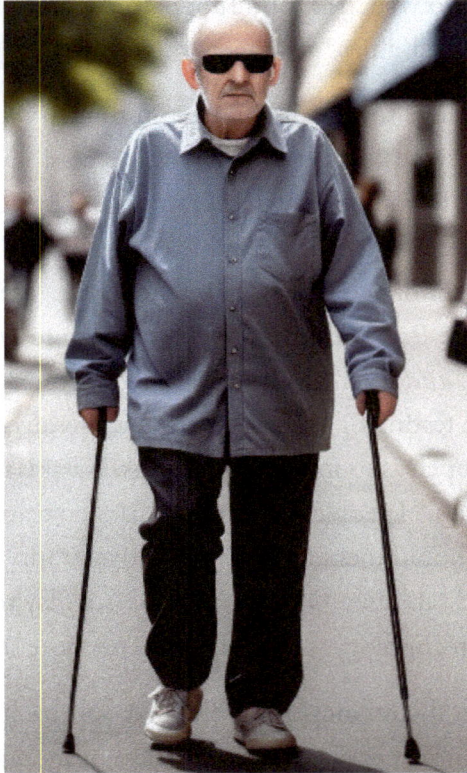

Image Description: An AI-generated picture of an elderly white male walking on a path, wearing a long-sleeved shirt and pants while holding canes in each hand.

Notice the overly broad assumptions and misrepresentations of this image. Faux black glasses, two canes that are nothing like the canes used by blind persons, and the supposition of the person being an older white male.

To create a more accurate image, I submitted a more sophisticated query.

Query Two: "A blind, mixed-race adult walking down the street with a white cane used by many people with visual impairments to navigate their environment. The white cane is straight, with no curved handle, and is roughly shoulder height. The person should not be wearing generic black glasses designed to hide their eyes but rather stylish glasses that fit their face."

Image 7: An AI-generated depiction of a blind female

Image Description: An AI-generated picture of a middle-aged bi-racial female wearing a dark sweater over a gray shirt. She appears to be walking across a crosswalk and is holding a cane in each hand, one white and one black and silver.

Notice that this image is better than the first, but still needs to be more accurate. Despite my more thoughtful, detailed query and description of the white cane, the image generator still could not correctly depict a white cane. In other words, CreateArt needs to be better educated on the accessibility tools used by disabled persons. The only way that happens is if people with disabilities use the tool more and if the community engages the CreateArt team.

If the disability community treats AI as a threat rather than an opportunity, no AI platform will be able to integrate a disability-centric mindset into its learning process. Thus, the risk is not AI itself. Rather, the risk is that AI continues to evolve and improve in a way that intentionally or unintentionally excludes persons with disabilities because it lacks sufficient feedback to grow and improve.

AI Is Here to Stay – So Deal with It

Because we are in a "gold rush" moment of AI, there remains a risk where technological advances become prioritized over user accessibility. The hope is that all those behind AI's constant innovation never lose sight of two facts established by the Centre for Inclusive Design:

1. If products and services are designed with unique needs, organizations can reach four times the number of intended consumers.

2. The relative cost of retrofitting a product or service to become inclusive will increase significantly over time. The cost can reach up to 10,000 times the product's price compared to introducing inclusive design principles earlier in the innovation process.[145]

Despite the challenges and concerns about AI, it will only continue to impact our personal and professional lives. It is the next steam engine, airplane, or printing press in the arc of human innovation. "Its capacity to multiply expertise, thinking ability, and knowledge means over the next decade we can significantly transcend human brain capacity," noted technology investor Vinod Khosla. "We're on the cusp of a near-infinite expansion of brain power that can serve humanity."[146]

Just as AI can serve humanity at large, it also can serve the disability community. As Yonah Welker, a public technologist, wrote in an article for the World Economic Forum, the most advanced AI in widespread use today – generative AI – "can support people with disabilities by fueling existing assistive technology ecosystems and robotics, learning, accommodation, and accessibility solutions ... [it also] ... can empower broader health and assistive solutions."[147]

Consider just a few of the AI-powered platforms that can help persons with disabilities for both visible and non-visible disabilities:

- Microsoft Seeing AI: Uses AI to describe people, text, and objects.

- Voiceitt: This platform is designed for people with non-standard speech and uses AI to learn and adapt a person's speech patterns so they can communicate easily.

- WheelMap: Uses AI to map and share information about wheelchair-accessible spaces.

- Predictable: Uses AI to predict text and phrases, which helps people with conditions like ALS or cerebral palsy communicate.[148]

For a more personal perspective on the impact of AI, consider how Austin Hanson, a non-verbal Paralympic athlete who represented the United States in the Athens, Beijing, and London Paralympic games uses Apple's AI-powered predictive text technology to assist him in communicating, "I use AI to listen in on conversations and provide ways for me to quickly interact. It's easy to get left behind in a conversation and most people don't realize how quickly they all bounce ideas and thoughts around to each other. This technology has really helped, and I know it will only get better."[149]

In other words, generative AI is already powering the four solutions identified by Chloé Touzet a few pages earlier. Given what generative AI is capable of, there is no telling what innovations and assistive solutions can come from the near-infinite expansion of brain power envisioned by Vinod Khosla as AI continues to advance.

Case Study: Using Generative AI to Make Documents Accessible

Most everyone is familiar with a PDF, the omnipresent format of documents intended to be hard to modify but easily shared, printed, or scanned. Most contracts and legal agreements are saved in PDF format – and there are an estimated three trillion PDF documents in circulation today. However, until recently, PDFs were not always accessible to persons with limited vision or blindness. According to Adobe – the creator of PDF – "Over 90 percent of the trillions of PDF documents in circulation today are at least partially inaccessible for individuals with disabilities, appearing blank, blurry or as lines of distorted text."

In May 2023, Adobe launched a new AI-powered "tagging" technology. This innovation "identifies structures including headings, paragraphs, lists, and tables – indicating the correct reading order for assistive technologies like screen readers. As a result, individuals with disabilities ranging from blindness and low vision to dyslexia can more easily navigate digital documents." Furthermore, the use of AI technology allows PDF owners to quickly and efficiently review large backlogs of PDFs to make them more visually accessible.[150]

Transformation #3: Rethinking Collaboration ... With an Accessibility Mindset

The emergence of AI across the economy is forcing many organizations to reconsider employees' roles and responsibilities. Every day, seemingly routine tasks are automated and, in some cases, transformed out of existence. As a result, "remaining work becomes more complex, dynamic, and creative, requiring higher levels of innovation and collaboration. Effective team dynamics become even more essential within and across teams."

AI is already in the process of taking over many data-intensive and easily automated roles in organizations. These include tasks like predicting what a particular customer is likely to buy, identifying credit fraud in real-time, detecting insurance claims fraud, and analyzing warranty data to determine safety or quality problems in automobiles and other manufactured products. We are familiar with AI-powered "chatbots" immediately appearing on service websites such as our bank or favorite online shopping platform.

While AI has automated specific tasks, it has also placed an even higher premium on tasks requiring creative thinking, brainstorming, and the use of so-called "soft skills" of interpersonal engagement. AI will never replace people in establishing a culture of ethics and inclusion, fostering face-to-face communications, and mentoring junior team members.

AI may also be a tool to accelerate innovation, but it cannot lay the groundwork for innovation to happen. Creativity, passion, and critical thinking are not things a computer generates. Harnessing those traits to drive innovation requires collaboration. Collaboration requires everyone to have a seat at the table, and ensuring everyone has one requires accessible, equitable professional environments.

In previous generations, the preferred model for generating new ideas or innovating was to bring a team together and require them to come up with a solution. The thinking was that by removing a group of people from the day-to-day distractions of their work, their creative potential could be unleashed, and ideas would flow freely. That practice rarely works. One Stanford Business School professor's study found that 71 of the 95 cross-functional teams created in 25 of the world's biggest companies failed to solve the problem they were assigned to address.[151]

Today, there is a lot more intentionality in problem-solving and brainstorming. There is a high degree of recognition of the importance of creating psychological safety and allowing for candor among diverse voices. However, the reality of achieving those important goals still needs to be revised. We can hold all the brainstorming sessions we want and create all kinds of intersectional teams. Still, if the way we work does not become more inclusive and accessible, psychological safety in the workplace is a mirage. With a universal feeling of acceptance in an organization, the creative passion and idea-sharing that underpins innovation will happen.

Remember that advancing collaboration and cultivating psychological safety also requires well-thought-out physical spaces. We all react differently to different types of built environments. Some of us need quiet, almost sterile settings so we can concentrate. Others feed off the energy of loud, energy-filled spaces where people are always congregating.

No matter how ambitious, the most important step in any process is to solicit feedback from the people using the space. Building on that, the space must be adapted to meet the needs of the greatest number of people. No venue will ever be perfect. But it can – and must – meet basic accommodations and accessibility needs for everyone.

Joseph Jones is the current Chief of Staff at the President's Office, Des Moines University, a medical and health sciences university located in Des Moines, Iowa (U.S.). Before that role, Jones was the Executive Director of The Harkin Institute for Public Policy and Citizen Engagement where he was instrumental in leading the design of the Institute's standalone building – arguably the most accessible building in the United States. Jones stressed the importance of incorporating accessibility and universal design into all physical settings to drive openness, collaboration, and sharing. Doing so requires leaders to be "Deliberate in actions, and proactive in thinking about the different types of spaces that people like to connect, whether it be a social or a work environment."

Jones continues, "You also need to think about creating varying types of spaces. There are times when you want to sit and be at a table and have focus. There are other times when you want to be in a space where you can have a great flow of conversation and good eye contact, and maybe even some closeness physically, to create that intimacy of conversation, and to build rapport that way. Other times there is value to having some wide-open space with clear lines of sight. And there always needs to be quiet, closed-off space where people are intentionally separated so they can focus."

Recognizing it is not always possible to have the resources to design and build the perfect space, there are common-sense steps that can be incorporated into almost any venue. As Jones said, "Start with the places that people most need or most often congregate. Places like entrances, bathrooms, and common areas are really important. Use colors and designs that are warm and welcoming. From there, you can move on to more ambitious projects when time and money permit."[152]

Rather than treating a workplace or even something like a meeting space for startups like an office, treat it like a destination where people want to come and be with others. Chances are, you will have a lot more success getting people to show up at an office that is universally designed and welcoming for everyone as compared to a sterile, inaccessible workplace.

Case Study: Senses Hub: A One-Stop Shop for Inclusive Innovation Across Africa

The challenges facing entrepreneurial efforts in developing regions are often exponentially greater than in North America and Western Europe. Cultural stigmas about disability are more significant, financial and social capital is scarce, and the distribution networks to bring products to consumers are often underdeveloped – or even non-existent.

Brian Mwenda, CEO of HopeTech, an assistive technology company, and several leaders in Nairobi, Kenya's disability community, joined forces to address those challenges. Their solution: Senses Hub, an innovation lab, convening venue, and office space all in one location, with a mission to drive disability-driven innovation throughout Africa. The Senses Hub team plans to replicate and scale the Nairobi location throughout Africa.

Consider the multifaceted approach to inclusivity offered by Senses Hub:

1. Assistive Technology Distribution Center: This center in Nairobi is a one-stop shop for state-of-the-art assistive technologies. From advanced digital aids to essential daily living tools, they ensure that cutting-edge solutions are accessible to those who need them most.

2. Research and Development: Senses Hub's research facility collaborates with global partners and focuses on the continuous development of AT solutions. The in-house team, equipped with the latest technology, continuously innovates and improves existing products.

3. Co-Working Space: The Senses Hub venue provides an accessible co-working environment where individuals and teams can collaborate, innovate, and bring their ideas to life. This space encourages creativity and networking among a diverse group of professionals and entrepreneurs.

4. Training and Workshops: Senses Hub is committed to education and empowerment. The team conducts regular training sessions and workshops on the use and benefits of AT to enhance skills and awareness.

5. Event Space and Networking Lounge: The event space hosts various activities, including workshops, seminars, and product launches.

6. Experience Center: Visitors can interact firsthand with various assistive technology (AT) devices, gaining insights into their functionality and impact. This hands-on experience is vital for understanding the potential of these technologies.

In addition to its physical location, Senses Hub actively advocates for disability-centric policies in Kenya and East Africa. For example, it is pushing for a tax exemption in Kenya for disability-centric products to make them more affordable for persons with disabilities. It also engages in trade policies among East African countries to improve the distribution of assistive technologies.

The Senses Hub leadership team is documenting the ongoing feedback it collects from users of the Hub to replicate the model elsewhere in Africa. The most important outcome of Senses Hub is the human connection it promotes. "We feel there's a need for a physical space where people come together," said Brian Mwenda. "We have really seen the impact of bringing people in the same room to discuss and share ideas. Sometimes we host accessible game events where you come and interact with people with disabilities and just spend time together. That always creates a lot of impact in all the participants, so I'm hoping we can have more of these centers across Africa."[153]

Image 8: Entrepreneurs Collaborating at Senses Hub

Image Description: Six people working at a table in the Senses Club building. They are collaborating on a project involving soldering electronic components. Photo credit: Derick Otormax

Transformation #4: Culture Matters – More Than Ever

No one is sure who made the famous statement "Culture eats strategy for breakfast" (assumed to be Steve Jobs or Jack Welch rather than Harvard Business School professor Peter Drucker whom the phrase is most often attributed to). However, there's no denying its truth. Put another way, before anyone – be it a head of R&D at a Fortune 25 company or a two-person startup working in a basement – can innovate a better product, they first need to innovate a better culture. Consider this statement from Stephen I. Sadove, the former chairman and CEO of several consumer-facing brands such as Saks, Inc.:

Culture drives innovation and whatever else you're trying to drive within a company - innovation, execution, whatever it's going to be. And that then drives results.

When I talk to Wall Street, people really want to know your results, what are your strategies, what are the issues, and what it is that you're doing to drive your business. They're focused on the bottom line. Never do you get people asking about the culture, about leadership, about the people in the organization. Yet, it's the reverse, because it's the people, the leadership, the culture, and the ideas that are ultimately driving the numbers and the results. So, it's a flip.[154]

No matter the legal protections, business opportunities, and well-intentioned goals of organizations to better understand disability, creating an inclusive, collaborative organization that accepts the ideas and experiences of persons with disabilities is impossible without a strong culture. Culture is the skeleton of any organization, and any weakness in the skeleton will bring down the entire structure.

It is culture – not formalized, legalistic disclosure practices or boilerplate press releases proclaiming support for things like National Disability Employment Awareness Month – that provides the safe space for employees to share – or not share – their disabilities and how their life experiences provide an opportunity for innovation. Culture permits people to utilize their diverse talents by proactively reaching out to colleagues or partners to brainstorm and think "outside the box" – to innovate.

Every employee, regardless of disability status, manifests the culture of organizations. In a 2021 *Harvard Business Review* article, Shanna

Hocking, a leadership development consultant, provided a helpful description of culture in the workplace:

> *At work, "culture" is a word used to describe the way people behave within an organization and the attitudes and beliefs that reflect those behaviors. It's the way people communicate, interact, and in general, work with each other. Leaders inform and create culture through the values, rituals, and rules they put into practice. It's what differentiates one organization from another, and can drive or diminish factors like inclusivity, flexibility, trust, and innovation.*[155]

Before the COVID-19 pandemic, organizational culture was assumed to always start at the top. The CEO and executive team set the tone and tenor for organizations, and employees looked to them for guidance, inspiration, and a sense of mission. In today's post-pandemic world, that is no longer the case. Culture is now more free-flowing within organizations, with all persons having a better ability to shape it.

The organic approach to disability inclusion is critically important to innovation. Yes, the organization's top sets the tone and the vision of success. Only the leaders can forcefully establish the value proposition of disability inclusion related to the organization's long-term success. The leaders bless the metrics of success and the key performance indicators to track progress.

Most importantly, the culture created by leaders must give every employee a sense of self-determination. Salary, performance bonuses, or the threat of losing a job are "extrinsic" motivators; self-determination is an "intrinsic" motivator. Extrinsic motivators only get you so much out of employees. People can be pushed only so hard before they burn out, no matter how much they are paid. Self-determination is part of creating an environment where "you get the best version of people," wrote Andy Walker, a frequent writer on organizational performance. This is where they are intrinsically motivated. When you get the best version of people you get people who throw themselves into the problem space."[156]

This new approach to culture has the potential to be far more resilient than the outdated model where culture was the sole responsibility of a few, and the rest were expected to accept it. "Importantly, this model doesn't relegate culture-building to an amorphous concept that everyone influences but no one leads or is accountable for," author and brand consultant Denise Yee Yohn wrote. "Shared responsibility for culture throughout an organization involves different people and functions within the organization playing different roles in developing and maintaining the culture."[157]

Maintaining a culture that embraces self-determination to maximize the talents of employees with disabilities requires "an all-hands-on-deck" mentality. The C-suite may set the vision, but mid-level managers have a high degree of responsibility to make that vision a reality, day in and day out. Supervisors must collaborate across the internal network to ensure reasonable accommodations are a given rather than an exception. Human resources teams ensure that hiring practices are accessible and collaborate with various external partners to bring diverse candidates into the recruitment process. Every employee takes a few moments each day to connect with their colleagues, learn more about their background, and offer help and compassion when needed.

Despite the challenges, an organic appreciation for the value of disability-driven innovation is the best way to shift from a "check the box, compliance-based approach to disability inclusion to one that is strategic and based on long-term value creation.

Case Study: Microsoft's All-Inclusive Business Strategy

Microsoft is a perfect example of a company taking an enterprise-wide approach to disability-driven innovation in a way that allows it to grow its market share. Arguably more than any other company in the world, Microsoft has integrated inclusion into every aspect of the business – physical design of its facilities, development of its workforce, product innovation, and sales and marketing. The company's commitment to "inclusive design" starts at the top – with CEO Satya Nadella. Nadella's oldest child was a legally blind quadriplegic with cerebral palsy. Nadella is very open about how "putting himself in his son's shoes" has "helped him see the need for Microsoft's products to be accessible to all and made him a more empathetic leader."[158]

Nadella "has made 'inclusive design' a core part of the company's business model. It is almost impossible to see a major Microsoft event or learn of a significant Microsoft announcement without hearing how accessibility is woven in."[159] Consider the various channels by which the company discloses its commitment to disability inclusion and the connection between inclusion, innovation, and advances in new product offerings:

- In recent years, Microsoft has continued to roll out accessibility features in its products, bringing innovations such as improved content sharing, more intelligent captioning and transcription features, and flexible ways to create content that are less reliant on traditional (and often inaccessible) tools such as keyboards.[160]

- In 2021, Brad Smith, Microsoft's President & Vice Chair, published an open letter entitled, "Doubling down on accessibility: Microsoft's next steps to expand accessibility in technology, the workforce, and workplace" that provided a detailed overview of Microsoft's plans to grow its business through inclusive design in its products and services. [161]

- Satya Nadella's letter to shareholders (i.e., investors) in Microsoft's annual report conveys the company's rationale for closing the "Disability Divide" – accessing the global market of more than 1 billion people with disabilities.[162]

- At Microsoft's 2021 annual shareholder meeting both Satya Nadella and Brad Smith made comments reinforcing the company's commitments on disability inclusion.

Without a doubt, Microsoft's focus on inclusion and accessible products is part of the strategy and vision set by the very top of the company's leadership – and their commitment is apparent. However, product innovation comes from the front-line employees taking that permission to create more inclusive products and reach more consumers. As Jenny Lay-Flurie, Microsoft's Chief Accessibility Officer, wrote, "Product inclusion starts by listening to ideas from diverse voices, especially disabled talent."[163] Lay-Flurie also pointed to Microsoft's accessibility features in its Windows platform, such as its Disability Answer Desk, which has supported over 1.5 million contacts with customers and employees.

Microsoft is also bringing its investors along on its journey. The leadership understands that without their support, the company will be unable to sustain ambitious commitments such as integrating inclusive design throughout its product offerings, devoting the resources necessary to develop an inclusive workforce, and providing over $2.5 billion in donated and discounted products and services. Through various communication channels and direct engagement with investors, Microsoft demonstrates that disability inclusion benefits the company, its shareholders, and society.

Disruption #5: The Politicization of Culture

Playing politics in the workplace has been around for thousands of years. "Work involves dealing with people, and people are, whether we like to admit it or not, emotional beings with conflicting wants, needs, and underlying (often unconscious) biases and insecurities," wrote Dana Rousmaniere in a 2015 *Harvard Business Review* article. "Our relationships with our colleagues – with whom we both collaborate and compete for promotions, for a coveted project, or the boss's attention – can be quite complex. Not everyone is friend or foe; many people are somewhere in between."[164]

Since 2016, however, workplace culture has become even more complex and challenging. In many world regions, electoral politics have become a flashpoint of tension among colleagues. Geopolitical conflicts such as Russia's invasion of Ukraine and the ongoing battle between Israel, Hamas, and Hezbollah have led to tense debates among colleagues and the belief that we need to take a side. Increasingly, people want to work for companies that "act with purpose." Consumers want to buy certain products and boycott others over political beliefs.

Despite the high stakes of the moment, no one knows what to do. "Leaders are struggling to respond to this new landscape, with some playing whack-a-mole on every issue and others simply ignoring employee criticisms in hopes they'll go away," wrote Alison Taylor, the author of *Higher Ground: How Business Can Do the Right Thing in a Turbulent World*.[165] More ominous, a global survey of 500 private sector executives by Herbert Smith Freehills (an international law firm) found that 46 percent of respondents believe employee activism is a risk. In contrast, only 20 percent see it as a benefit. A whopping 97 percent of respondents indicated their organization either has implemented or is considering placing "moderate to high restrictions" on employee activism (such as joining public protests, signing petitions, and posting online content).[166]

These findings are disconcerting for several reasons. Without exceptional care and thoughtfulness, attempting to stifle or regulate employee actions and voices threatens free speech in many countries worldwide. Further, such actions risk derailing the carefully curated cultures in many organizations. It flies in the face of reality to think organizations are living their cultural mantras about creating safe work environments where everyone is valued when potentially strict limits are imposed on what employees can do or say. It also is evident that employees with disabilities are particularly sensitive to limits – real or perceived – on how employees are allowed to share thoughts and opinions in the workplace.

Adapting to a New Workplace Dynamic

The disruptions of the past few years have been a mixed bag for everyone. There is much optimism and many reasons for hope that, ultimately, many disruptions will promote more inclusive and innovative work environments. However, the downside risks are real and will not go away.

In the coming chapters, we will explore the concepts of innovation and transformation in greater detail. Creating and maintaining a culture of innovation is the most difficult challenge for any organization, regardless of its size or mission. Nortel, Nokia, Toshiba, and even Blockbuster were once hailed as being on the cutting edge of innovation. Today, they are either gone or – at best – barely hanging on to relevance. Countless startups claimed to have an innovative idea but either could not turn it into reality or found the market was too crowded and complex to break into. Innovating is hard. Innovating to a point where you initiate a transformation is almost impossible.

Even more daunting, the journey is getting more complicated, not easier. For all the reasons we covered in this chapter – and many more we did not – it is even more challenging to achieve innovation and reach transformation today than thirty years ago, when the Sony Walkman was the prized possession of many. Yet there are building blocks that organizations can stack together to move meaningfully and intentionally toward a place where we all have opportunities to use an innovative mindset to transform how we live, socialize, and work.

Case Study: CareSource: Measuring Progress for Accountability and Impact

CareSource is a non-profit company that provides managed healthcare to over 2 million members across the United States. In January 2023, CareSource embarked upon a substantial effort to incorporate competitive, integrated employment at all levels of the organization. The Purpose Statement of its disability inclusion work underscores CareSource's commitment to becoming a model employer, "Promote disabilities as a positive and natural part of the employment experience and to become a model employer for people with disabilities."

CareSource's disability inclusion strategy falls into three objectives, each with a series of specific workstreams to achieve their Purpose Statement:

1. Build a sustainable disability-inclusive culture

   - Culture and Leadership
   - Accommodations, Enterprise-Wide Access & Benefits
   - Employee Data and Disclosures
   - Training and Education

2. Attract, grow, and retain employees with disabilities at every level

   - Recruitment and Hiring (including new hire experiences)
   - Training and Education
   - Employment, Retention, and Advancement (including internal mobility and promotion in the organization)

3. Establish CareSource as an industry leader in disability inclusion

- Community Engagement and Partnerships
- Supplier Diversity
- Markets
- Brand Reputation

"Our approach is comprehensive, reaching nearly every aspect of our company and our employee lifecycle," said Patrice L. Harris, CareSource's Director of Diversity, Equity, and Inclusion. "We broke down the work to align with and address our three main objectives to ensure we make continual progress towards each one. The workstreams are comprised of people whose jobs align with their assigned workstream and associated deliverables. To increase engagement and commitment, it was important to minimize the work being done "off the side of their desks." This way, we are blessed with the expertise of each workstream member, while they get credit for their efforts to support our disability inclusion strategy."

Through its enterprise-wide commitment, CareSource treats disability inclusion as a competitive advantage in the market. As Erhardt Preitauer, President & CEO of CareSource, has asserted, "At CareSource, our employees, members, and providers of all abilities are what sets us apart. We believe building a diverse workforce makes us a stronger and more successful company."[167]

Making the connection between advancing disability inclusion and achieving business outcomes, Solomon Parker, Director of Intellectual and Developmental Disabilities at CareSource, stressed, "As a healthcare company, it is essential our workforce is aligned with the demographics of CareSource's member population and that our employees fully appreciate the health care needs of all members."

Led by Patrice L. Harris and Solomon Parker, the company has implemented several best practices to become a fully disability-inclusive company. Of note, CareSource has:

- Engaged in research about best practices of competitive, integrated employment within its industry and among companies such as Microsoft and JPMorgan Chase, which are recognized leaders.

- Conducted extensive internal research to gather employee feedback about their experiences at CareSource and what CareSource can do to continue to foster an inclusive environment.

- Established a large, cross-functional team of internal leaders, experts, and persons who identify as disabled. This action committee is divided into the ten workstreams noted previously that encompass CareSource's disability inclusion efforts.

- Created the National Disability Inclusion Advisory Board (NDIAB), a group of 10 independent experts in disability employment (all of whom either identify as disabled or have a close, personal, and/or professional connection to disability) to advise CareSource on its efforts. The NDIAB meets with the CareSource team every quarter and is available to provide input and feedback as needed.

An important lesson quickly learned by the CareSource team was the vital importance of executive support. Said Parker, "The first few times we brought the team together were rough. People were coming together from across the enterprise. No one was sure about how much CareSource invested in disability inclusion. Which meant they were unsure of how much they wanted to invest in themselves. Once it became clear that Patrice and I were empowered to drive results, people came on board. I would not say any of this has been easy, but we have made a lot of progress."

Because of the expansive nature of CareSource's commitment across the company, the team developed an internal "dashboard" to track deliverables and progress to ensure key performance indicators (KPIs) are met. The dashboard also flags deliverables that appear to be lagging or; behind schedule so action can be taken to address them.

The dashboard provides both a macro and micro perspective of progress. Whereas the main page of the dashboard is the "big picture" CareSource also tracks progress by each workstream, Image 9 provides the detail of where progress is tracked along specific tasks within the three main objectives. These images depict the progress of each workstream in 2024.

Image 9: CareSource Disability Inclusion Dashboard — Objective-Specific Pages

Objective 1: Build a sustainable disability-inclusive culture

- 90% — 1. Culture & Leadership
- 81% — 2. Accommodations, Enterprise-Wide Access & Benefits
- 93% — 3. Employee Data and Disclosures
- 83% — 5. Training / Education

Objective 2: Attract, grow and retain employees with disabilities at every level

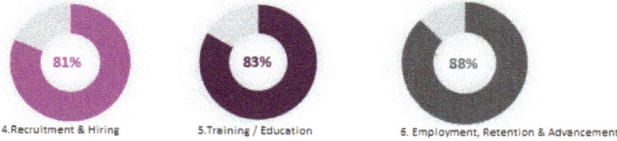

- 81% — 4. Recruitment & Hiring
- 83% — 5. Training / Education
- 88% — 6. Employment, Retention & Advancement

Objective 3: Establish CareSource as an industry leader in disability inclusion

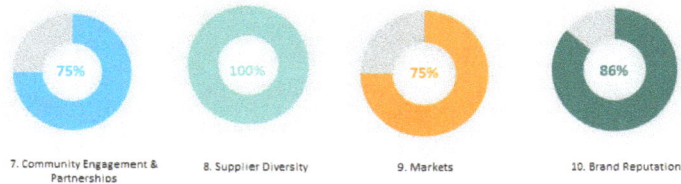

- 75% — 7. Community Engagement & Partnerships
- 100% — 8. Supplier Diversity
- 75% — 9. Markets
- 86% — 10. Brand Reputation

Image Description: A series of ten pie charts aligned with the workstreams created by CareSource to implement its approach to achieve its purpose statement of becoming a model employer for people with disabilities.

Behind the dashboard are a series of detailed datasets that serve as an ongoing repository for all information related to the disability inclusion initiative. These provide real-time status updates, allowing Harris and Parker to understand the work and promptly give updates to all relevant stakeholders.

"If I could give one piece of advice to leaders in disability inclusion, it would be to ensure the work is always aligned with the business," said Harris. "We spent a lot of time with our executive sponsors and leadership making sure we were measuring the right things and tracking the data in a way that is in line with our operations. I know I said I had one piece of advice, so this next one is free. Another piece of advice is to prioritize progress over perfection. Don't wait until you have the "right" level of support or the right people on your team. Don't get discouraged if your journey is slower than others – just keep moving, keep building, and keep creating a more inclusive work environment for everyone!" [168]

CHAPTER 7

Innovating to Transform

Change never happens at the pace we think it should. It happens over years of people joining together, strategizing, sharing, and pulling all the levers they possibly can. Gradually, excruciatingly slowly, things start to happen, and then suddenly, seemingly out of the blue, something will tip.

—Judy Heumann, an internationally recognized disability rights activist, widely regarded as the mother of the Disability Rights Movement.

As is obvious by now, two words used throughout this book are "innovation" and "transformation." Thus, it is essential to define these words well and better understand how the concepts of innovation and transformation interact with each other in practical terms.

With the explosion of technology-driven solutions over the past decade, the concepts of innovation and transformation have taken on a new meaning – albeit one that is not entirely accurate. A simple Internet search demonstrates that both are increasingly associated with a narrow purpose of digital technology – the electronic tools, devices, and systems that process, transmit, and store data in binary form (zeros and ones).[169] The Internet, servers, routers, and cloud storage are all digital technologies. Companies have spent billions – perhaps trillions – innovating and transforming their IT systems. Law firms and consultancies have entire practice areas dedicated to helping their clients manage digital transformation and innovation.

Innovation and transformation are also often associated with business operations. Daily, we learn of a business "transforming themselves" to meet changing consumer needs or adapt to the latest market trends. However, that notion misses the point. Innovation and transformation have much broader meanings and broad applications in our lives. They can occur within us as individuals, in our communities, and across networks of friends, family members, and collaborators. In his seminal research, *Diffusion of Innovations*, Everett M. Rodgers clearly asserts that innovation goes far beyond the hardware of technology, "We often think of technology mainly in terms of hardware. Indeed, sometimes the hardware side of technology is dominant. But in other cases, technology may be almost entirely composed of information: examples are a political philosophy such as Marxism, a religious idea such as Christianity, a news event, a policy such as a municipal smoking ordinance."[170]

Thus, Archer Acher's innovation of a campaign to increase accessibility in his school or building more curb cuts in sidewalks has the potential to be as impactful as any computer, router, or server.

Through research and conversations for this book, I learned that innovation and transformation primarily occur along two tracks:

1. Institutional – ideas generated by employees of a company or organization to make better products, drive market opportunities, and increase profitability. Another term for this is "intrapreneurial," which refers to employees or close associates acting as internal entrepreneurs by taking the initiative within the company's structure to innovate. An example is Amazon's release in May 2024 of AI-powered upgrades to its Fire TV software. Amazon says that the AI-powered functionality enables users to "search for TV shows and movies using natural prompts and phrases, and you can search by topic, genre, plot, character, actor, or even by quote." Having something approaching a

conversation with Alexa helps get around dips in a person's cognitive abilities. Instead of trying to remember the names of movies or shows, you can ask Alexa to show you all options based on a genre or character.[171]

2. Entrepreneurial – ideas generated by entrepreneurs or micro-enterprises, often ad-hoc, low-budget, and experiential. Many times, this form of innovation in the disabled community is driven by necessity. Unable to find employment in the formal economy, persons with disabilities often become entrepreneurs and start businesses in search of professional and personal fulfillment.

Case Study: Appreciating How Entrepreneurial Innovation Makes the World Better

An example of entrepreneurial innovation is Marianne Dijkshoorn's work. In 2014, Dijkshoorn founded Welkom Accessibility & Events, a Netherlands-based company that helps organizations produce events and conferences accessible to all attendees. Dijkshoorn was forced to become an entrepreneur. It was not her first calling. Dijkshoorn could not find a job in a traditional employment setting when she began her career. She was classified as "enough" disabled by the Dutch government. Still, her disability was deemed not to be severe enough for potential employers to qualify for a government subsidy for employing her. Once potential employers learned that Dijkshoorn was disabled, but they would not receive a subsidy for hiring her, the potential employers moved to other job candidates.

As Dijkshoorn said, "I had the feeling of discrimination a lot of times. Sometimes, I had temporary work, but when the contract was extended, I had to leave again because employers were convinced to place a subsidized person in this position. The only way these companies would hire a disabled person was if they got a subsidy. These jobs were often also specially created jobs for people with disabilities, and it was not about whether you had the best qualifications for this job. So, I had the feeling the system was against me. I had to find another way to show my talents and to earn money to live on."

The final push to becoming an entrepreneur came when she wanted to attend the Subconscious Festival with friends. The festival was on a steep hill that she couldn't walk, and the hill was too steep to do in a wheelchair. She asked the organization how she could enter, and they asked her for advice. So, the next year she made Subconscious the first festival accessible in the Netherlands.

From those unfortunate beginnings, Welkom Accessibility and Events has become very successful. Welkom Accessibility and Events has several corporate clients; she has collaborated with the Tour de France Femmes (the world's most prestigious women's bike race), TwitchCon Europe 2024, The National King's Day 2023 in Rotterdam, and the Eurovision Song Contest 2021 to make the venues accessible to people with physical, auditory, visual, and cognitive disabilities. Finally, Dijkshoorn wrote *Make Your Event Accessible for Everyone*, a book with practical and straightforward tips to make events accessible for everyone.

Dijkshoorn also makes customized "Wheelchair Mats" that designate specific spots for wheelchair users, ensuring comfort and safety. The mats are available in two sizes and can be designed in various colors and brand schemes. Through her innovative creativity, Marianne transforms events into accessible venues that are welcoming to every attendee.

Her innovation journey took work. She started working on the Wheelchair Mat concept in 2019. Just as business started to pick up, the COVID-19 pandemic hit, shutting down all in-person events for almost two years. Marianne had no investors, advisors, or immediate customers – just her and her husband.

Yet, Dijkshoorn persevered. By 2022, business started to pick up. She now sells her mats to restaurants, event organizers, and individuals using wheelchairs. Dijkshoorn has a mix of ready-made and custom-designed mats, which can be stored in a protective tube when not in use. To date, she has sold close to 1,000 mats all over Europe. She also finished second in a national competition to be the Netherlands' "Freelancer of the Year Award."

The Wheelchair Mats have two important outcomes. First, the mats can provide educational moments for people. As Dijkshoorn recounted when her mats were used in a concert hall, "One time someone watching the concert walked up and stood on the wheelchair mat. They did not realize what the mat meant. Another visitor asked them, 'Do you know what you are standing on? Do you know why that mat is there?' That person looked down and saw they were on a wheelchair mat. They then understood why the mat was there, and they moved away."

Image 10: A Wheelchair Mat produced by Marianne Dijkshoorn

Second – and most important – the mats are a great equalizer. The mats allow restaurant guests a more accessible and accommodating meal experience. If you place the mat correctly, a wheelchair user will have an equal hospitality experience during every leisure activity. They allow people attending meetings to appreciate that everyone is welcome and has a seat at the table – a mindset like creating accessible parking spaces. "It's been a journey," said Dijkshoorn. "But I am so happy because my work makes the world more inclusive, especially for people with a disability."[172]

Understanding Innovation

Innovation traits are consistent across cultures, regions, industries, and people – not just disability-driven innovation. Persons with disabilities must understand and utilize these ingredients, as any other person wants to innovate and transform beyond the status quo.

Let's return to the definition of innovation developed by James Phills and his colleagues at Stanford University. They characterize innovation as a process or outcome that meets two criteria. "The first is novelty: Although innovations need not necessarily be original, they must be new to the user, context, or application. The second criterion is improvement. To be considered an innovation, a process or outcome must be either more effective or more efficient than preexisting alternatives."[173]

Manifold, an advisory and early-stage investment firm, has developed a compelling Venn Diagram that places innovation in the context of value, novelty, and solutions. As Image 11 indicates, innovation is the center of all three traits, and all three must be part of the innovative process.

Image 11: A Visual Depiction of Innovation[174]

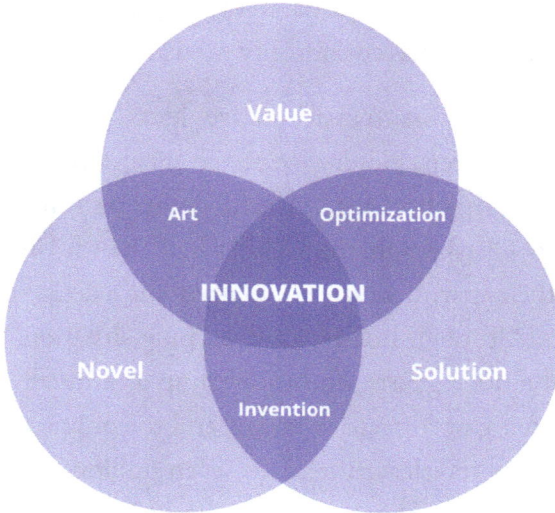

Image Description: A Venn Diagram with three interlocking circles (Value, Solution, Novel). The area where all three circles intersect is labeled Innovation. The places where circles intersect are labeled Art, Optimization, and Invention.

As previously noted, the innovation's scale or reach is irrelevant. What is relevant is the level of improvement or value it creates, be it for a single person or an entire consumer segment. An innovation's reach and impact must not diminish the fact that any innovation that allows for improvement compared to existing alternatives is, in fact, innovation.

Innovation can be something as momentous and enduring as the typewriter. It can also improve a company's online job portal to make its job application and career recruitment process more accessible. Innovation can also be a business, such as Ashton Gilbert's UnBoxed Recycling. From conception in March 2021 through December 2023,

Ashton and his company recycled 175 tons of cardboard in Wilson County, Tennessee (U.S.). UnBoxed Recycling is also firmly committed to the Wilson County community as it often donates cardboard to emergency moving situations and local non-profit community gardens. Consider that, in 2023, UnBoxed Recycling donated over 6 tons of cardboard boxes to address community needs.

Even the greatest, most transformative ideas come from humble beginnings. As Lauren Landry wrote in Harvard Business School Online's Business Insights Blog, "Airbnb got its start in 2007 when co-founders Brian Chesky and Joe Gebbia had the idea to rent out air mattresses in their apartment to people attending a design conference in San Francisco. Although not an ideal sleeping situation, it was 'good enough' for the three guests who showed up and much cheaper than staying in a hotel. Fast forward to today, and the online vacation rental marketplace offers travelers more than seven million accommodations and 50,000 experiences from around the world."[175]

In each case, the innovation improved previous practices. The typewriter is far more efficient than pen and paper. Marianne's company and her Wheelchair Mat make for better human experiences. UnBoxed Recycling diverts hundreds of tons of cardboard from landfills to recycling or other practical uses. Airbnb provides people with more flexibility and enhanced lodging options when traveling.

Nurturing and Scaling Innovation

There are five key ingredients to creating a culture of innovation. First, employees and entrepreneurs must be empowered to experiment, think big, and generate ideas. Everyone needs encouragement to go beyond the status quo – whether they work in a Fortune 500 company or are entrepreneurs working in their garage. People will only think big when the culture around them – personal or professional – is conditioned to allow them to think that way.

Second, and building on the first ingredient, innovators must feel comfortable bringing their authentic selves to their work and the innovation at hand. This book has explained extensively the importance of getting one's authentic self to work. The same is valid on the individual level and in our personal lives. It doesn't matter where the innovation is occurring or its motive – we all need to feel comfortable and supported in who we are to do our best work.

Third, leaders must avoid institutional silos and what often comes with them – breakdowns in communications and excessive layers of bureaucratic decision-making. In a *Harvard Business Review* article about innovation in organizations, Fabrizio Salvador and Fabian Sting identified a common pitfall: "Employees seldom perceive their idea's evaluation and selection as transparent, and often it is unclear why an idea received low scores or has been rejected. And although frontline employees are best positioned to sense changing business conditions and opportunities, they are generally the least heard (because they are at the lowest level of the organization)."[176] While small-scale startups do not have the same silos as larger organizations, the fact of the matter is ensuring that all those involved in the process have an opportunity to engage in the feedback loop is a lesson that applies broadly.

Fourth, there must be transparent, two-way communication around innovative ideas. All employees have the right to know promptly and constructively if their ideas are on the right track and to be part of the decision-making process for the concept's outcome. The same applies to small-scale innovators. Their network of friends and advisors is responsible for giving timely, honest feedback.

Fifth, there must be resources dedicated to innovation. Innovators need time, support, and, in many cases, financial backing to generate ideas and bring them to fruition. Writing from personal experience, it's an exercise in frustration and futility when trying to innovate a new product without adequate resources. While no one should be given a blank check, innovating on the cheap or trying to piggyback innovation off the sale of other product offerings seldom succeeds. At best, a minimum viable product (MVP) concept is deployed in the market. However, innovation rarely scales beyond that on a shoestring budget. Even worse, anything less than a total commitment to innovation causes the entire team to feel deflated and at odds with one another. Emotions are raw, and frustrations are undeniable. The executives believed adequate resources were given, but the team needed to be more creative and work harder. The team feels let down by the lack of financial support and is confident that the product would have been successful if a last investment injection had been made.

In every organization (and in the network of supporters of every "lone wolf" innovator), there must be an honest conversation and a clear set of expectations very early in the process. Nurturing and scaling innovation cannot be a Fool's Errand. If these five ingredients are not in place, innovation will invariably come up short and disappoint. The stories of persistence and overcoming incredible odds in the face of adversity make for great books or movies but those stories are the rarest of exceptions. For every Steve Jobs and Steve Wozniak, there are millions of entrepreneurs whose ideas did not make it in the market. The reality is that innovation occurs against genuine constraints, which must be acknowledged and dealt with daily.

Building a Culture of Innovation Is Not Fun ... Or Easy

In a 2019 *Harvard Business Review* article, Harvard Business School Professor Larry Pisano provided a frank assessment of what it takes to create an innovative culture. He interviewed hundreds of executives. Virtually every one of them said they wanted to work in an organization defined by innovative culture. Further, as Pisano noted, every one of them "readily provided a list of characteristics identical to those extolled by management books: tolerance for failure, willingness to experiment, psychological safety, highly collaborative, and non-hierarchical. And research supports the idea that these behaviors translate into better innovative performance."

Yet, creating a culture embracing those traits is a rarity.

According to Pisano, the reason is:

> *... innovative cultures are misunderstood. The easy-to-like behaviors that get so much attention are only one side of the coin. They must be counterbalanced by some tougher and frankly less fun behaviors. A tolerance for failure requires an intolerance for incompetence. A willingness to experiment requires rigorous discipline. Psychological safety requires comfort with brutal candor. Collaboration must be balanced with individual accountability. And flatness requires strong leadership. Innovative cultures are paradoxical. Unless the tensions this paradox creates are carefully managed, attempts to create an innovative culture will fail.*[177]

Understanding Transformation

Where innovation involves a narrower set of collaborators and a relatively immediate timeline, transformation is slower-moving and systemic. Transformation is a culmination of a single or many innovations on a broad, interconnected scale. Innovations may or may not endure. In contrast, "Transformation is a profound, fundamental change, altering the very nature of something. Transformational change is both radical and sustainable. Something that is transformed can never go back to exactly what it was before."[178]

The best ideas or innovations become transformational because they transcend time, geography, culture, and industry. The typewriter may have transformed how we communicate, but it has not transformed society. The typewriter innovated how we put words on paper. The iPhone also transformed how we communicate; arguably, it has transformed society, given everything an iPhone can do. The iPhone brought together multiple innovations – writing, speaking, information sharing, content creation, data management, health monitoring, and navigation, to name a few. The typewriter was a huge step forward in helping visually impaired people communicate, but it cannot compete with an iPhone regarding all the technologies to be deployed. The typewriter is the text function of the iPhone. It does not have the iPhone's web browsers, email, image detection features, or ride-hailing apps. How persons with disabilities engage with technology and use it daily will never go back to what it was before the iPhone.

Image 12 is a helpful illustration of how an idea or an innovation impacts society to become part of a broader transformation. The Democracy and Human Rights Education in Europe initiative developed a similar visual along with providing a helpful description of how ideas and innovations move through society: An idea starts at the bottom left and "spreads and grows at the interface with others: To like-minded people, then to larger networks around these. It enters a journey through different circles connected in different ways. Along the way, it can change and can change these other areas or sectors."[179]

Image 12: How an Innovation Moves Through Society

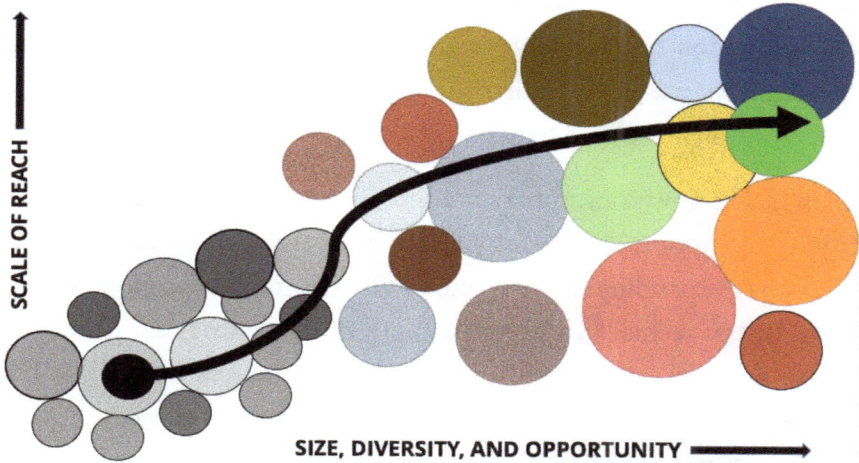

Image Description: A chart depicting a trendline of innovation through society. The Y axis is labeled "Scale of Reach," and the X axis is labeled "Size, Diversity, and Opportunity". Image created by Robert Ludke.

As the idea or innovation appeals to more people, it moves into increasingly extensive and disparate networks. The connections between the actors are looser and more differentiated. However, the reach and size of the actors are much more significant as the idea progresses.

Think of Apple's many innovations in this journey. The original Apple product was a "motherboard" created in a garage in 1976 by Steve Jobs and Steve Wozniak. It was an add-on to other computers and only appealed to a niche group of computer hobbyists in the San Francisco, California area. Those hobbyists were very homogenous — a tightly connected group of enthusiasts united by their love of computers and technology.

Then, Apple brought the Apple I to market, followed by the Apple II and Apple III. After that, there were many iterations of the Macintosh and the MacBook. Apple's ability to transform society accelerated in the 2000s with the iPod, the iPhone, and the iPad. No single Apple product by itself transformed how we live, work, communicate, and innovate. It is the entire constellation of Apple products that created the transformation. At each stage of Apple's innovation, the company had to communicate the product's value proposition to the market – otherwise, buyers would have gone to competitors.

With each innovation, Apple's products moved more and more quickly from a core group of early adopters to an ever-larger market of buyers across ever-expanding societal sectors. What started as a product used by a handful of techies in California evolved into a product line sold to people from all backgrounds, for myriad uses, across the world. The competition may eventually overtake Apple, but we are never returning to what life was like in 1976.

The Importance of Critical Thinking

As demonstrated, much disability-driven innovation and societal transformation are borne out of necessity, if not outright desperation. No magic skill set is required, and disability-driven innovation is not limited to a select few experts with advanced degrees. What is most important is the life experience that can creatively solve a problem.

A successful approach to disability-driven innovation and transformation contradicts what most believe to be the engine of innovation in today's economy. An inclusive approach that values different ideas and lived experiences is critical to innovating and turning the innovation into a viable product.

Unfortunately, too much innovation comes from narrow thinking done by people with homogenous backgrounds who cannot apply different lived experiences to solving challenges. As Greg Satell forcefully wrote:

> *Management fads usually come from people who did well in school.*
> *Many of these are business school professors and consultants, who've*

never operated a business. They are often people who've never failed, been told that they're smart all their lives, and expect others to be impressed by their ideas, not to examine them thoroughly.

They tend to come up with their ideas by talking to other smart, successful people about their experiences. These ideas get picked up by more smart, successful people and are propagated further. The elite hivemind then puts these ideas into practice, rarely checking what evidence the ideas are based on. When the ideas fail, they are rarely questioned. Shortcomings are blamed on poor execution by less smart, successful people.[180]

Contrast Satell's characterization of closed-minded and insular thinking with thinking driven by diverse groups of people from different backgrounds. In a November 2016 *Harvard Business Review* article, David Rock and Heidi Grant observed:

Working with people who are different from you may challenge your brain to overcome its stale ways of thinking and sharpen its performance. Diverse teams are more likely to constantly reexamine facts and remain objective. They may also encourage greater scrutiny of each member's actions, keeping their joint cognitive resources sharp and vigilant. By breaking up workplace homogeneity, you can allow your employees to become more aware of their own potential biases - entrenched ways of thinking that can otherwise blind them to key information and even lead them to make errors in decision-making processes.[181]

Taking the concept of an inclusive approach to innovation and transformation to another level, we add on the experiences and perspectives of persons with disabilities...that inclusivity is the difference between the "fad" mentioned by Satell and sustaining an innovation to a point where it becomes transformational.

The Most Important Ingredient for Success: Networks

Reid Hoffman, the Founder of LinkedIn, provided a great point of context for every entrepreneur and business owner. "One of the things that's important for business leaders to do is think broadly about what their responsibilities are. Because businesses are not just these little, abstract, profit-generation machines. They're things that live within networks. They live within networks of customers, networks of employees, networks of investors, and society."[182]

The truth is that despite the powerful examples in this book and countless others across society, disability-driven innovation has not yet transformed the world into one that is inclusive, equitable, and accessible for everyone.

As this book has already covered, there are many reasons preventing disability-driven innovation from transforming society. There are also many reasons that innovation has not transformed society for the better.

The least understood and appreciated reason for innovation's inability to scale to transformation is a failure to understand the importance of networks – multilateral connections between people, communities, organizations, policymakers, and every sector of the economy. Reid Hoffman's quote is relevant because it reminds us that the entrepreneurship of disability-driven innovation is just one piece of the global economy and just one segment of an interconnected network of actors.

Consider this powerful passage from Mark Somerfield, someone who identifies as neurodivergent and one with more than 20 years of experience as a chief technology officer in startups and early-stage companies:

> Over the years I've worked with or consulted with many startups and small businesses with varying degrees of success. I can count some that have successfully sold their businesses to achieve capital exit, or

attained a sustainable and consistent level of profit; I can count others that have crashed and burned and folded or continued to subsist in a kind of zombie state, chewing up investor money without ever really coming close to making it. My current business is on life support but we're probably one angel investor away from break-even.

Among these cases, I see zero correlation between the methodological or technical competence of the founders and senior leadership and the success/failure outcome of the business. At best, committed and skillful adherence to the lean methodology has served to prolong the inevitable, but all of the success stories have been primarily founded on one thing:

Relationship-building.[183]

Somerfield asserts that the point of differentiation between success and failure in innovation is relationships. Having a network of partners, customers, and investors to provide an entrepreneur with investment capital, access to more customers, and other resources is more critical than the innovator's talents or even the innovation's merits. You can have the best-conceived idea, but it will fail if no one knows about it or can support its growth.

Consider the partnership between the alliance between the Montana Department of Labor & Industry, Great Falls College, local employers, and Montana Vocational Rehabilitation and Blind Services that created an accelerated, 6-week Structural Welding course. In recent years, the State of Montana (U.S.) has found itself in increasing need of skilled professionals in the welding industry. It is estimated that Montana will need 220 new welders every year over the next five years.

The program is designed to prepare individuals with little to no experience for a career in welding. The jobs are more than entry-level, and the starting salary is about $50,000.

The course is designed to accommodate students of all backgrounds and personal commitments. Each cohort has 26 students, and enrollees range from single mothers to recent high school graduates to persons with disabilities.

Montana Vocational Rehabilitation found that careers in automotive skillsets—including welding—are exciting to graduating high school students and its clients throughout the state.

Montana Vocational Rehabilitation (the State of Montana's program that assists persons with disabilities in obtaining and maintaining employment) participated in the partnership because skills like welding are more than a job – they are a pathway to independence and self-sufficiency for persons with disabilities. As Chanda Hermanson, Montana's Administrator of Disability Employment and Transition Division, said, "This initiative empowers individuals with disabilities by opening doors to independence and meaningful employment while rapidly earning family-sustaining wages. It showcases the strength of our community when we work together."[184]

An example of collaboration to scale impact globally is Zero Project's Scaling Solutions. First launched in 2018 under the name "Zero Project Impact Transfer" by Zero Project, a Vienna, Austria-based global initiative to support the implementation of the Convention on the Rights of Persons with Disabilities (CRPD), the Scaling Fellows Initiative focuses on transferring and advancing innovations for entrepreneurs with disabilities to new countries and regions by offering individualized scaling support.

Zero Project Scaling Solutions is notable for three reasons:

1. Diverse and Impactful Partners. Zero Project has convened a global team of collaborators to help expand the initiatives' effectiveness and reach. The Essl Foundation and Fundación

Descúbreme backed the Zero Project Impact Transfer. As the Scaling Fellows Initiative has grown, so has the number of collaborators. Notable partners include Deutsche Gesellschaft für Internationale Zusammenarbeit (GIZ) from Germany, the multinational IT company Atos, and Inclusive Creation, an IT consultancy firm based in Norway. Indian NGO EnAble India joined the program partners in 2024.

2. Social Capital. Social capital is just as essential as financial capital to the success of an enterprise or an innovation. The social capital provided to the "Scaling Fellows" who are part of the Scaling Solutions initiative includes individualized support, training, mentoring, networking, and increased visibility through the Zero Projects various events, publications, and communications channels.

3. A Cross-Sectoral Network. Beyond the partners in Scaling Solutions, Zero Project has established a global network of more than 10,000 experts, policymakers, corporations, academics, and other persons with and without disabilities. Such a broad and diverse network allows Scaling Fellows to tap into a truly diverse network of ideas and lived experiences, along with the ability to replicate their solutions on a global scale.

The intentional effort to create a massive network to support disability-driven innovation is borne out of the reality of innovation. "Innovation does not just happen by itself," said Robin Tim Weis, the Director of International Affairs at Zero Project. "Innovation is developed through extensive collaboration across the public, private, and nonprofit sectors. To advance disability-driven innovation, we need global platforms for identifying, sharing, and disseminating effective solutions that remove barriers faced by persons with disabilities."[185]

Case Study: Building Networks to Innovate

Sandy Lacey, the Executive Director of the Howe Innovation Center at the Perkins School for the Blind, has made a career at the intersection of entrepreneurialism, venture launching, and disability-driven innovation. In particular, she has spent years analyzing the networks of people and organizations involved in the market for disability technology innovation. Lacey has three actionable insights and recommendations for how innovators and entrepreneurs can launch and scale a venture in the disability market.

First, create a blueprint for building a company. "One of the big myths of entrepreneurship is that people are winging it," said Lacey. "The fact is you cannot just wing it. You need a plan. You need an approach, and you need to be able to show people how, exactly, you are going to follow through on your idea." Lacey said she always refers to *Disciplined Entrepreneurship*, a book by Massachusetts Institute of Technology (U.S.) professor Bill Aulet. *Disciplined Entrepreneurship* contains 24 steps every entrepreneur should follow to create and scale a successful startup venture.

Second, join a startup accelerator program for entrepreneurs and business venues. "Many provide basic business and entrepreneurial coaching as part of their program. Some of them are much more competitive than others. But if you start at one that is not as competitive, you'll learn a ton, and it will position you to be in a much better place to then get accepted into one of the more competitive programs," suggested Lacey.

Third, build a network of outside advisors. Said Lacey, "Find a loose group of two to four people who are entrepreneurial veterans within your community. Someone who has a vested interest in your success. They might care about your entrepreneurial success because of the type of entrepreneur you are. Maybe it is a school connection, maybe it is people in your neighborhood or a local investor group. You just want a committed group of people willing to be a sounding board and able to give you advice on taking your ideas to the next level."[186]

Lacey's recommendations point to an underlying truth about building a business – entrepreneurs make their own luck. Successful enterprises don't just happen. The essential ingredient to making luck is actively engaging others in the journey. Mark Manson, a multiple *New York Times* #1 best-selling author wrote it best: "Lucky people enjoy connecting and relating to other people and are comfortable doing so. When presented with new social situations, unlucky people talked to people they already knew or people who were most like themselves, whereas lucky people talked to a large array of people equally."

Manson shares a life lesson for all of us, "Most of life's opportunities don't land on us mysteriously. They come through our networks, our connections, and people we stumble across at random."[187]

Every person and organization has a network. Networks are comprised of people and organizations sharing ideas and information through all forms of communication – meetings and conversations, social media, attending or participating in conferences, and so on. We engage in networks because they empower us to deploy our expertise and resources to pursue an outcome, such as disability-driven innovation. In a way, networks are "force multipliers" of our pursuits. They are the infrastructure through which we exchange ideas and turn ideas into products or services to create a more equitable and inclusive society.

Networks have been around since humans started interacting with one another. As notable historian Niall Ferguson wrote, "Networks are the spontaneously self-organizing, horizontal structures we form ...These include the patterns of migration ... that have distributed our species and its DNA across the world's surface; the markets through which we exchange goods and services; the clubs we form, as well as the myriad cults, movements, and crazes we periodically produce."[188]

The challenge is for us all to constantly grow and improve our networks. The best networks are a mix of tight connections – people we trust and collaborate with – and loose connections – an organization that hosted your startup at a conference. Lacey's recommendations for building a business include tight connections (the two or three people serving as advisors) and loose connections (the relationships formed by participating in an accelerator program). Those connections evolve – loose connections at an accelerator program's start might become tight connections over a few months of collaborating. Advisors may leave the venture and be replaced by others.

An example of how Sandy Lacey and her colleagues built a network to advance disability-driven innovation was its #HackDisability: AI for Accessibility Hackathon, which occurred in February 2024. The Howe Innovation Center at Perkins School for the Blind convened students from 11 universities at MIT's CSAIL (Computer Science and Artificial Intelligence Laboratory) for a weekend of human-centered design innovation. Mentors from over 30 companies like Amazon, McKinsey, Vispero, LinkedIn, Google, Cisco, and others gathered to guide the students, with all mentors having the lived experience of disability and/or deep expertise in accessibility and design. All volunteered to spend the weekend working in small teams to innovate new technologies to help people who are blind or have low vision access more of the world. Starting at 6 p.m. on a Friday, the ten teams had until noon on Sunday to identify, design, build, and test their new products before presenting to a panel of judges for a chance to win $2,500 to further their research and development. Their products had to be explicitly focused on using artificial intelligence.

To succeed, each group had to bring together various lived experiences. People were out of their comfort zones as many were meeting for the first time – and suddenly had to collaborate. To maximize their innovative potential, the teams had to create from scratch a culture that had an appreciation for failure, a willingness to explore, and a balance between psychological safety and honesty.

In addition to cash incentives provided by Amazon, the teams were encouraged to continue collaborating with the possibility of displaying the prototype out of the event on the floor of Boston's Museum of Science. The outcomes were both impressive and potentially transformational. Within those 40 hours over a weekend, the groups "hacked" on everything from indoor wayfinding (because GPS doesn't work inside) to emotional interpretation to figuring out how to help blind people make infographics for their professional presentations.[189]

Case Study: A Partnership to Reimagine the 21st Century Workforce

In 2013, Mike Hess founded the Blind Institute of Technology (BIT) to reduce the unemployment rate for the blind and visually impaired community.

"One of the greatest untapped human resources on the planet is the blind and visually impaired community and broader disability community," said Hess. He speaks from personal and professional experience. Hess became blind at a young age, and his professional career encompassed years as a highly-paid software engineer in the telecommunications sector.

With a mission of "making employment opportunities digitally accessible to all and ensuring that every individual, regardless of disability, can find meaningful employment that aligns with their skills and aspirations," BIT is a global nonprofit staffing and recruiting agency. Central to achieving its mission are BIT's two Registered Apprenticeship programs for the blind and visually impaired to gain workplace experience in the software industry.

Since 2013, BIT has served over 600 professionals collaborating with leading companies including Randstad, JPMorgan Chase, Salesforce, CVS Health, Ball Corporation, and Allstate.

Its most significant and impactful partnership is with Salesforce – a global software company with nearly $35 billion in annual revenue and consistently ranked as one of the best companies to work for in the world.

In early 2020, Salesforce launched its Workforce Navigators program to support job candidates with disabilities interested in careers within the Salesforce ecosystem.

When Sarah Mark, Director of the Workforce Navigators program at Salesforce, learned about BIT, she contacted Hess to explore a potential collaboration.

"Well before the pandemic, BIT was holding Salesforce trainings for people who are blind and low vision," said Mark. "During and after the pandemic, several organizations approached us to collaborate on developing trainings, but BIT already had a training module in place. That's when we recognized the best course forward was to develop a partnership and help expand the impact of their work."

The partnership has had a profound impact over the past four years: 141 job seekers have completed training (26 Salesforce have been certified), and 33 have been employed.

Salesforce and BIT are not content with a status quo mindset in the partnership. Hess and Marks are collaborating to ensure participants in the Workforce Navigators program have the skills to build a long-lasting career. "This is not about getting people an entry-level job," said Hess. "The partnership is about giving people skills they can use for a meaningful career, no matter where they work."

The size and scope of the trainings also continue to expand. The organizations are exploring how AI can further help narrow the disability employment gap.

Mark has some lessons for others to consider as they build and scale partnerships with disability-driven innovation at their core. "First, you have to find a partner that is committed to the work," stated Mark. "We knew that, because BIT was already doing Salesforce trainings, Mike and the team had a vested interest in our success. Second, create metrics at the front end of the engagement and socialize them with all parties so people know what to expect when it comes to the potential impact and outcomes. And third, storytelling is how you get people engaged and supportive of a partnership. Yes, data is important. But the stories are how you connect with people. We have a lot of great content on our Workforce Navigators website. We know that site visitors most appreciate the stories of the people making the change happen in society."[190]

CHAPTER 8

Creating Markets for
Disability-Driven Innovation

*Almost always when you find something really
cool for people with disabilities, it will find its
way into the mainstream in a way that is
wonderful and makes life better.*
—Dr. Joshua Meile, a blind adaptive technology designer and recent
recipient of a MacArthur Foundation "genius" grant

I published *Transformative Markets in April 2020*. The book's premise is that the only way to scale goods and services created with a more sustainable future in mind – wind and solar power, electric vehicles, and upcycled clothing, to name a few – is to harness the power of markets.

We use markets every day. Amazon and Instacart are markets. Markets determine the price of gasoline. The bartering between tourists and street vendors in Nairobi, Kenya, is a market. Ticket prices for a Taylor Swift concert are set by markets (although many believe the prices and availability are unfairly manipulated by bad actors in the market).

Prices for goods and services are determined through interactions between buyers and sellers, which in turn impacts the forces of supply and demand. While we most often encounter a market's endpoint (the grocery store or an online shopping site), supply and demand drive how goods and services are invented, made, priced, and mass-produced worldwide.

While there is no such thing as a perfectly functioning market, the reality is that markets are the only force in society strong enough to solve systemic challenges such as unemployment and underemployment across the global disability population. We do not have a better, more viable economic model waiting to be deployed. As noted in Chapter 4, public policy has done an adequate job setting a floor that helps protect the civil rights of persons with disabilities and provides a social safety net. However, we cannot characterize public policy as a consistent, meaningful driver of disability-driven innovation or, more fundamentally, the employment of disabled people. Most troubling, in the more than 30 years since its enactment, the Americans with Disabilities Act (and similar legislation in other countries) has done little to fundamentally change the employment status of persons with disabilities.

As noted in Chapter 2, many current policies are too often an impediment. The private sector often treats disability inclusion as a compliance mandate or philanthropy initiative rather than an investment strategy. Investors are on the sidelines and not yet the forceful advocates they could be for competitive, integrated employment. Nongovernmental organizations (NGOs) representing the disability community cannot consistently exert their influence to drive lasting change in disability employment.

In contrast, markets are a powerful tool waiting to be utilized. As I wrote in *Transformative Markets*, "There is one force powerful enough to spur change at the rate we need by balancing the realities of life as we know it: markets. Driven by good old-fashioned supply and demand, markets create opportunities every day in every part of the world. Markets are the mechanisms by which the ideas of innovators are brought to life and made available to consumers."[191]

Or, as Pulitzer Prize-winning author and journalist Tom Friedman asserted in his best-selling book *Hot, Flat and Crowded*, "The only thing that can stimulate this much innovation in new technologies and the radical improvement of the existing ones is the free market. Only the market can generate and allocate enough capital fast enough and efficiently enough to get 10,000 inventors working in 10,000 companies and 10,000 garages and 10,000 laboratories to drive transformational breakthroughs; only the market can then commercialize the best of them and improve on the existing ones at the scope, speed, and scale we need."[192]

But ... Markets Are Imperfect

While markets may be the only force able to achieve systemic change across society, there is no such thing as a perfect market. A perfectly functioning market exists only in theory. Buyers and sellers never completely align on a price that perfectly matches the value of the inputs (namely human talent, money, and natural resources) and disruptions (natural disasters, monopolies, recessions, poor government policies, and so on) that often occur, thereby introducing imbalances to the market.

Perhaps the most crucial caution about markets was offered by Rabbi Jonathan Sacks, who astutely noted, "The market economy is better at producing wealth than at distributing it equitably."[193]

Advocates for accelerating the use of markets to drive disability-driven innovation must acknowledge those imperfections. We must understand their flaws to improve how markets work.

It is impossible to think we can create a market in which every human talent is maximized; there are zero government subsidies, no bad actors trying to control the market, and people are paid for their worth. Unfortunately, too many people are exploited in our market-based economy. However, we can (and must) get much closer to markets that better use our different lived experiences and human and natural resources in a way that creates more innovation. Without a dramatic acceleration of disability-driven innovation, we're all consigned to a less productive, more resource-scarce, and increasingly inequitable future.

Despite the urgent need for more disability-driven innovation across every market in the global economy, no one should presume to have the power or the influence to force wholesale changes in the behaviors of billions of people. No one wants to be told what to do. Discrimination will always exist. Government policy will never be precisely tailored to our needs. Securing financing will always be challenging. Some people will – unfortunately – always be marginalized in a global economy.

Yet, there is no viable alternative. No other economic model has sustained itself, and we certainly cannot invent a newer, better economy on the fly. Most importantly, the opportunity to utilize the existing markets to accelerate disability-driven innovation is too great to pass up. Despite the barriers and challenges, we need to work with the markets we have today and commit to improving them.

Improving the Markets of Today for a Better Tomorrow

The best first step in improving markets and accelerating the growth of disability-driven innovation is to change our mindset about the role of markets in society. Too often, we treat markets as a distant concept like Amazon – a giant conveyor belt that can get us what we want when we want, no matter the price. Too often, when we buy something, we want our immediate needs met. We don't spend much time or energy thinking about how the products are made, their environmental cost, or whether the people who made the products are paid a living wage. In our mind, the cheaper and faster we get it, the better.

Instead, we must expect more from markets. Markets must create things that add real value to our lives. It is the difference between buying a cheap t-shirt at a fast fashion store for a few dollars that we wear once and throw away versus spending more money to buy a shirt from Patagonia or North Face that is made with recycled materials and can be worn for years.

It is the difference between designing and building houses that work only for able-bodied people and building homes that are open and accessible to all. From a long-term value creation standpoint, building a new house that only appeals to a narrow group of people makes no sense. Instead, a more successful housing market would be built on universal design principles – things like wider doors, open floor plans, and more accessible bathing features – and can be used by everyone. An accessible house also stands the test of time as its owners age and lose mobility. The more people who can use the housing, the more units will be sold. This will lead to a more vibrant and profitable market than one that caters to fewer buyers.

The good news is that improving markets is not impossible. It is well within our ability to enhance current markets and create new markets that create value for us all. Unlike other economic models that rely heavily on central governments for their direction, "Capitalism can be quite malleable," observed Andrew Hoffman in *a Stanford Social Innovation Review* article. "It is designed by human beings in the service of human beings, and it can evolve to meet the changing needs of human beings. This has happened throughout its history to address issues such as monopoly power, collusion, and price-fixing."[194]

Even more promising is that Hoffman believes we are in the early stages of a market transformation. We are shifting from markets driven by intense resource consumption – be they environmental, social, or financial – to ones that operate much more in line with society's future needs.[195] Gone are the days of coal mining and all the societal costs that came with it. Our energy increasingly comes from cleaner, more efficient sources of energy that require skilled technicians to build and install. In other words, now is the time to bring greater awareness of disability-driven innovation's value proposition to policymakers, entrepreneurs, investors, and companies worldwide.

The Global Market Opportunity for Disability-Driven Innovation

Return on Disability Group estimates the most accurate and credible assessment of the global market for persons with disabilities. To restate some of the Return on Disability Group data shown in Chapter 1, the market opportunity is enormous. For example, 22 percent of the population identifies as having a disability – which is approximately 1.6 billion people. If you factor in family and close friends, the market becomes 63 percent of the world's population with an annual spending power of over $18 trillion.[196]

When you consider three critical factors, the market opportunity for disability becomes much more significant than what is estimated by the Return on Disability Group. For example:

- People are often temporarily disabled through illness, injury, or life experience, yet they do not consider themselves disabled.

- People with disabilities are not always comfortable disclosing their disability and thus are not accounted for in official statistics.

- It is common for people with disabilities to be unaware of their disability and, thus, are not accounted for in official statistics.

Given those factors plus the intersectional nature of the disability, one can make a convincing argument that the global disability market is the worldwide population (slightly more than 8 billion),[197] and its value is equal to that of the worldwide economy (roughly $105 trillion).[198]

Although that assertion may be overly aggressive, the global market for disability-driven innovation includes billions of people and is worth tens of trillions of dollars – and will only increase in size and value over time.

That is not to declare that every innovator or entrepreneur with a disability must have a mindset or a business model to tap into a global market for their product or service. Innovation and entrepreneurship are impressive no matter their scale or reach. The point is that the market opportunity for disability-driven innovation is massive in scale, and disability-driven innovation must never be treated as a narrow segment of the economy or merely a niche market. It does not matter if you are a solo entrepreneur providing accessible website design consulting services to small businesses or if Elon Musk is transforming a sector of the global economy. The opportunity is there.

Case Study: Creating a Pipeline for Disabled Talent to Become Sports Commentators

In October 2023, NBC Sports and Making Space launched a partnership to collaborate to identify and develop on- and off-camera employment opportunities for Disabled talent for NBC Sports' coverage.

An immediate priority of the partnership was providing NBC Sports with on- and off-camera talent in time for the Paris 2024 Olympic and Paralympic Games.

Making Space is an accessible talent acquisition and learning experience platform that develops new pathways to employment and career advancement for Disabled talent. Its goal is to provide the necessary resources and opportunities for Disabled people to create meaningful careers and become influential leaders.

A key component of the partnership is free and accessible training co-created by NBC Sports and Making Space. The training brought together a group of aspiring Disabled on-air talent for a week of intensive, Disabled-led training at the NBC Sports Studio in Stamford, CT. Additionally, they filmed a course that is hosted on Making Spaces' talent acquisition and learning platform to create free and accessible opportunities at scale, the online course focuses on the basics of sports television commenting with a disability-centric focus. Starting with a foundational knowledge of models of Disability and person-first language, course participants advanced through modules focused on interviewing techniques, scriptwriting, mastering teleprompter use, and building on-camera confidence.

Students who completed the course entered NBC Sports' talent pipeline. Course graduates could showcase their skills by uploading a showreel to the platform, putting them in the "pre-qualified" applicant track for NBC Sports. Once in the pre-qualified applicant track, the candidates are considered for opportunities by NBC Sports.

Disabled talent who were hired through this program for the broadcasting of the Paris 2024 Games marked the first-ever Disabled Hosts of the Paralympics for NBC.

"Through our partnership with NBC, we've learned the importance of consistent communication across teams to maintain alignment and momentum," said Keely Cat-Wells, CEO of Making Space. "We've also seen that integrating initiatives into broader organizational priorities, rather than treating them as standalone projects, ensures sustainable impact and seamless execution."

Separately from their work with NBC Sports, Making Space served as Consulting Producers for the LA28 Paralympic Handover event, where its team provided paid mentorship and employment opportunities for

Disabled talent, awareness and language training, guidance on inclusive hiring, creative and editorial input, and advice on set design and production logistics.[199]

The Actors in Any Successful Market

Markets for goods and services do not happen alone. No one person or company can create a significant, lasting market for a product or service without the involvement and collaboration of other market actors.

Consider, for a moment, Tesla.

Electric vehicles had little appeal to consumers 15 or 20 years ago. However, since 2008, Elon Musk and Tesla have pursued a borderline obsession to simultaneously reinvent the electric vehicle and reimagine how we use transportation. Legacy auto manufacturers only embraced the idea of electric vehicles once Tesla started eating into their market share in 2020 and after. Tesla is proving that consumers want – and like – electric-powered vehicles of all kinds – automobiles, SUVs, school buses, and even e-bikes. Had it not been for Tesla, the traditional auto industry would never have deviated from its century-old, deeply entrenched addiction to manufacturing petroleum-guzzling vehicles powered by polluting internal combustion engines.

Despite Tesla's perseverance through a long journey of innovation and the cutting-edge innovation behind the vehicles, Tesla did not succeed independently. Tesla is a product of collaboration by a varied group of market actors. In their own way, each supported Tesla and the global infrastructure the company needed to survive, let alone grow. Tesla needs more than just roads for its cars and trucks to drive on. It requires a functioning legal structure in many countries to protect its intellectual property and facilitate contracts; employees must be educated and trained, and a financial system that allows people access to credit to purchase Tesla's vehicles.

In *Transformative Markets,* I noted that the only way a market lasts over time and can transform a part of the economy is when four critical actors in the market come together in collaboration to develop and maintain it through a balance of generating profits and meeting the public good:

1. Public Sector (the "Enablers"): policy and regulatory officials at all societal levels – from local mayors and city councils to the United Nations - that establish the legal and regulatory framework for domestic and international markets. The public sector also provides the educational foundation to train Tesla's employees and give them the lifelong skills they need to succeed in their jobs.

2. Private Sector (the "Builders"): those that bring the expertise and infrastructure (namely manufacturing facilities and supply chains) to engage in the production of whatever goods and services are needed by society.

3. Cause Sector (the "Validators"): foundations like the Ford Foundation, academic institutions, and not-for-profit organizations such as the World Resources Institute that bring expertise and credibility.

4. Finance Sector (the "Financiers"): those that supply the financial capital needed to fund the private sector's innovation and provide the resources needed to turn the innovations into actual products, such as development banks like the World Bank or Asian Development Bank, investment firms, venture capitalists, and other types of banks.[200]

Underpinning the interaction of the above market actors is the idea that every successful product or service in every market must accomplish one thing: meet a human need. It does not matter what that product is – shampoo, an iPhone, an electric vehicle, food, or coffee sold in a local coffee shop. If a product does not address consumers' needs, no one will buy it. And if consumers are not buying something, there is no market for it. It's that simple.

The best innovators can create something that meets a human need and build (or tap into) a network of collaborators to help scale a market. Because they must constantly innovate in an inaccessible world, innovators with disabilities are skilled at meeting human needs. These range from bendy straws (think about how many millions of parents have used a bendy straw to help their young children take a drink) to audiobooks.

The best part about markets driven by innovation is they beget more innovation as the value creation that comes from them leads to more opportunity, more ideas, and better means of production.

Image 13: The Virtuous Cycle of Innovative Markets

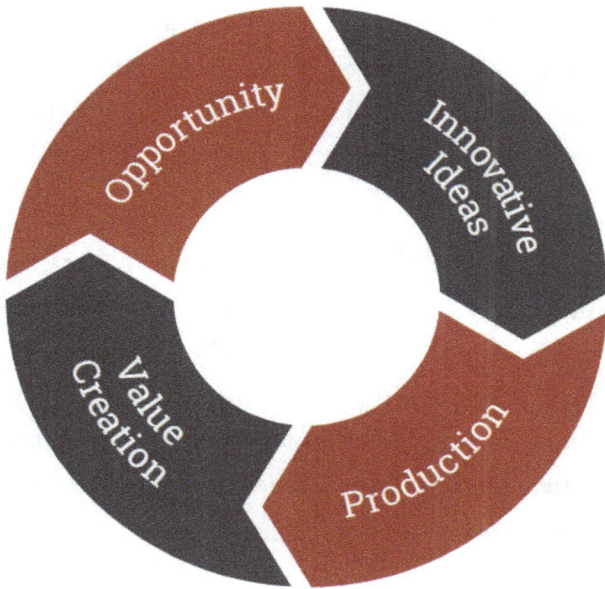

Image description: Four curved arrows that create a connected, continuous cycle of innovation. The arrows are labeled Value Creation, Opportunity, Innovative Ideas, and Production. Image created by Robert Ludke.

The Market Forces Behind the Rise of Tesla

Suppose we apply the lens of the market actors to Tesla. In that case, the company has benefitted from each actor bringing their expertise, connections, and resources to create a market for electric vehicles. Elon Musk was behind the company's efforts to sell the vision of an EV future to these actors, and he must be commended for bringing them together and harnessing their influence. One can question his methods, motivations, and successes (or lack thereof) in other areas of his business empire. Still, give credit to Musk and Tesla for permanently disrupting the stodgy and entrenched auto industry.

Consider the roles played by the various market actors:

- Public Sector. Tesla has benefited enormously from the public sector. Governments in every one of Tesla's markets provide it with immeasurable resources, such as an educated pool of talented workers, infrastructure (roads, bridges, vehicle charging stations, and parking lots), and legal frameworks that help protect the company's intellectual property from competitors.

Tesla has also received direct and indirect financial support from taxpayers. In the United States, this support ranged from tax credits available to consumers purchasing electric vehicles to payroll assistance during the COVID-19 pandemic (readily taken by Tesla while Elon Musk was publicly criticizing government support for individuals) to $1.3 billion in tax incentives provided by the State of Nevada to help Tesla build a battery factory in the state.[201]

- Private Sector. Tesla has leveraged many meaningful partnerships with companies like Panasonic (the co-creator of the battery factory in Nevada), Mercedes Benz (collaborator in developing the sophisticated driver assistance sensors in every Tesla model), and Daimler (an early-stage investor in Tesla and technology partner).[202] Tesla opened its earliest large-scale manufacturing plant in Fremont, California. The facility is a 5.3 million-square-foot factory that Toyota and General Motors previously owned.[203]

- Cause Sector. Tesla's engagement with the cause sector includes both conflict and cooperation. On one side, some significant cause sector organizations, such as the World Wildlife Fund and Sierra Club, have strongly criticized Tesla over the environmental risks in its supply chain. At the same time, the company has ample support from industry groups such as the Electric Vehicle Association, Plug In America, Global Battery Alliance, and the Fair Cobalt Alliance.[204]

- Finance Sector. Musk invested roughly $70 million of his own money in Tesla. Other early-stage investors in Tesla included Abu Dhabi's Al Wahada Capital Investment, Valor Equity Partners, and VantagePoint Venture Partners – all of whom were handsomely rewarded on the first day of Tesla's IPO with a 40 percent return on their initial investment.[205] The financial returns have been even greater for those who have held the investment since Tesla's IPO.

So, Why Aren't There More Market Transformers Like Tesla?

Excellent question! Much of Tesla's success can be attributed to factors outside its control. As noted, a global framework of policies, financial capital, and human expertise was available for Tesla to maximize its market opportunity. Tesla also has the benefit of timing. Yes, any successful entrepreneur knows when the market is ready for his or her product. But Tesla was able to meet the moment because the necessary infrastructure was in place for it to do so. Tesla would have withered if it had started ten years earlier when no one was paying attention to EVs. Beginning in 2000, the Toyota Prius hybrid – despite being described as an "over-styled cheese wedge"[206] – opened consumers' minds to more fuel-efficient transportation. Around 2010, the growing climate crisis finally started entering consumers' consciousness. Plus, government policymakers were far more receptive to the idea of supporting EVs in 2015 than they were in 2005.

Unfortunately, Tesla's massive success in improving a global market worth trillions of dollars is an exception, not the norm. There are three primary reasons we have been unable to create markets that transform society for the better – be it for goods and services built with sustainability and responsibility at their core or for those innovated by persons with disabilities.

First, the interests of every actor in a market rarely align. In a paper published in *Industrial Marketing Management*, four Finnish professors found that actors in markets for sustainable products may be united in a common goal – achieving a more sustainable society – but are often faced with a complex mix of different timelines, competing motives, diverse perceptions of risks and responsibilities, and various roles in creating products. In other words, the critically important cross-sector collaboration around EVs produced by Tesla is a rarity in markets, not the norm. Unless all the actors involved in markets for disability-driven innovation begin to work more closely and purposefully, market growth will be stunted.

Second, as covered in Chapter 1, development silos often stifle cross-sector collaboration and innovation. When people and organizations are overly focused on maximizing their potential in their narrow market segment, the mindset becomes one of competition instead of collaboration. That myopic approach stifles innovation and hinders its ability to transform.

Third, there are what I call "externalities" that distort markets or serve as a disincentive for their growth. In more traditional markets, externalities are monopolistic practices or supply chain breakdowns. Externalities in markets focused on innovating a more inclusive society include outdated public policy, social stigmas, marginalization, and physical barriers such as inaccessible work environments. Starting any business is challenging. It is even more complex when structural barriers serve as powerful disincentives. Those barriers are precisely what is hindering the collaboration needed to scale markets for disability-driven innovation.

Five Essential Ingredients for Scaling Disability-Driven Innovation in Markets

In May 2023, The Harkin Institute for Public Policy and Citizen Engagement held a two-day summit that brought together entrepreneurs at the forefront of disability innovation, private sector executives, policymakers, and investors for a series of conversations about how to scale disability-driven innovation.

Here are five lessons in collaboration taken from the summit, along with deeper insights from Global Disability Innovation Hub's (GDI Hub) work in scaling entrepreneurship and innovation in the assistive technology sector:

1. Social Capital Matters – A Lot

    Entrepreneurs need mentors, collaborators, and opportunities to bring their goods and services to market. Without social capital, every business – no matter its value proposition – is doomed to fail.

    This need is especially critical in emerging markets where disabled people often face higher levels of stigma and discrimination, which limit their social circles and connections for partnerships.

2. Financial Capital Is Not Reaching Entrepreneurs with Disabilities

    Accessing financial capital is a struggle for every entrepreneur, regardless of disability status. Those challenges are exacerbated for entrepreneurs with disabilities, in part due to a corresponding lack of social capital. Financial capital is virtually non-existent for entrepreneurs without access to a solid and influential social network.

    Too often, venture funding opportunities in these regions come from charity-model mentalities. While charity and philanthropic funding have important uses, they have also been known to stifle capital investment and market growth for assistive technologies.

3. We Must Better Communicate the Intersectional Nature of Disability Innovation

Rather than seizing upon disability's intersectional nature, too often the value proposition of disability-driven innovation is conveyed as appealing to only a niche population. As a result, too many efforts to help spur entrepreneurship among underserved communities or populations take an overly narrow approach to defining entrepreneurs.

Organizations and funders focusing on supporting innovators who are veterans, people of color, women, LGBTQ, low-income, and other marginalized populations without making these programs accessible and inclusive of entrepreneurs with disabilities are missing large numbers of innovators within their target populations. We needlessly stifle innovation that provides comprehensive benefits by taking a narrow approach to the innovative potential of disability-driven innovation.

Investors must also better embrace this intersectionality and celebrate the social impact of diversity-first investment, which can deliver significant impact alongside financial rewards. Disability-driven innovation allows investors to create long-term value for themselves and society.

However, none of this can continue to be a secret. As a result, it is incumbent on the disability community to communicate the value proposition and the everyday reach of disability-driven innovation more actively. It is a fact that disability-driven innovation is taken for granted. Like it or not, the burden of communicating that value proposition falls on those who stand to gain the most from advances in disability-driven innovation.

4. Disabled People are Problem Solvers – So Empower Them!

For persons with disabilities, innovation is often a matter of necessity and survival. Imagine the influx of new ideas at a company where twenty to thirty percent of its workforce was empowered to bring their best, most authentic selves to work daily. Imagine the value that could be created if those employees were permitted to apply creativity, resourcefulness, and resilience to their jobs rather than spending time and energy masking their disability.

5. Supply Chains Are Game Changers

Because of scarce social and financial capital, many disabled-centric innovations never become part of the supply chains of large companies. Yet those supply chains represent enormous opportunities for disabled entrepreneurs to grow and scale their products and services. Unless organizations take a more expansive and inclusive approach to creating diverse supply chains, disability-driven innovation will not reach its full potential to create lasting benefits for society-owned enterprises. It will be consigned to – at best – niche markets in the global economy.

Globally, import and export duties and processes must be improved in venture growth, especially in emerging markets. Balancing this are examples of country-specific assistive technology distributors unlocking supply chains alongside the design and development of innovations.

Case Study: Global Disability Innovation Hub: Creating Markets for Disability-Driven Innovation

Headquartered in London, England, Global Disability Innovation Hub (GDI Hub) GDI Hub is a research and practice center with a mission of "Driving disability innovation for a fairer world." GDI Hub operates in over 40 countries and works with more than 70 partners from all sectors of the global economy. Its impact is lasting and expansive. GDI Hub has an investment portfolio of more than £50 million and has reached 37 million people since its launch in 2016.

A key reason for GDI Hub's impact is its ability to bring together the four types of actors in the global economy that are vital to making markets for goods and services. As GDI Hub notes, one of its differentiators is its unique way of scaling disability-driven innovation, "Transformative outcomes can be achieved by doing things differently. We bring together the coalitions that others haven't, to lead new thinking which can overcome intractable barriers to participation."[207]

A significant market of focus for GDI Hub is launching, mentoring, and funding ventures in the AT markets in developing countries. The ventures supported by GDI Hub range from wheelchairs and prosthetics to eyewear and digital devices. The importance of increasing access to AT in developing countries cannot be understated. As GDI Hub has found, "The scale problem is also compounded by poverty; 80 percent of people who need AT live in emerging markets. Disability is also a cause and consequence of poverty."

The core of GDI Hub's efforts to expand the AT market is providing African entrepreneurs and innovators with the necessary financial and social capital. GDI Hub's AT Impact Fund was set up to provide financial capital (in the form of grants) alongside social capital (technical expertise, mentoring, and business management skills) to help AT ventures in Africa overcome the challenges of creating a market offer and scaling their offer within Africa.

The creation of the AT Impact Fund – as part of the GDI Hub's UK Aid – funded AT2030 program, was driven by a glaring weakness GDI Hub found in Africa's AT market, "Historically markets have not existed for AT and therefore have been filled by the work of non-governmental organizations (NGOs), which have developed local and global mechanisms of scale, but require continued grant funding to maintain supply for the growing demand. There is also an undesired knock-on effect, in that the market fails to emerge as the demand is being met by 'free at point of delivery' services."

In other words, AT innovation and market growth in Africa have been stifled because of poor market dynamics. Rather than the four actors necessary to grow and scale a market – the public, private, cause, and finance sectors – Africa's AT market has historically been driven by the NGOs in the cause sector. As a result, AT innovation and entrepreneurship have lacked the necessary interplay with other market actors. There are few essential relationships with policymakers to create a conducive regulatory environment. The private sector is not helping provide scalable and lasting access to large numbers of consumers, and the finance sector is not injecting the all-important financial capital into AT innovation and development.

An example of GDI Hub's ability to help scale a business to address disability is its collaboration with Wazi. Started in Uganda, Wazi is an African social enterprise focused on providing affordable and accessible eyecare solutions. It operates eye clinics and conducts eye camps to provide eye tests and glasses to people in need. Wazi's mission is urgently needed. According to the World Health Organization, "One in every six blind people globally live in Africa, along with 26 million others grappling with some degree of visual impairment."

One reason for that pervasive disability is that the market for sophisticated assistive eyecare technologies and everyday eye care products in Africa is not functioning well. Consider this assessment by AT2030, an organization backed by GDI Hub, "Key market barriers that perpetuate the current situation of low access to eyeglasses in [low and middle-income countries] include low levels of investment by governments; high costs to the end-users; complex in-country supply chains; a service delivery model that requires high levels of resources in terms of personnel and infrastructure; limited number of points of services and sales; and low awareness and acceptance of eyeglasses."[208] All of these factors point to a failure across market actors to collaborate and invest in Africa's eyeglasses market.

Through the Assistive Tech Impact Fund – and GDI Accelerates, the startup accelerator arm of GDI Hub – Wazi gained access to the market actors necessary to grow and increase its market share while helping people in East Africa access low-cost yet reliable vision care.

Consider what Wazi gained from its participation:

- Mentorship and Expertise: GDI Hub connected Wazi with experienced mentors and industry experts who guided product development, business strategy, and market entry.

- Funding: Wazi received financial support from the program, which enabled them to scale their operations and expand their reach in Africa.

- Networking Opportunities: GDI Hub facilitated connections with potential investors, partners, and customers, helping Wazi build a strong network within the disability tech ecosystem.

- Market Access: GDI Hub's extensive network and resources helped Wazi navigate the African market and identify new growth opportunities.

The Assistive Tech Impact Fund (ATIF) tested and proved the fundamental hypotheses that catalytic capital combined with expert venture strengthening and market access can cultivate the ideal conditions for AT ventures to find a pathway to scale in LMICs. ATIF, and programs like it, are building the scaffolding and the bridges to make access to affordable and high-quality AT a reality for millions of people.

Despite the proliferation and growth of innovation ecosystems and venture support programs in LMICs, persistent systemic barriers still hamper establishing the AT sector as a credible destination for large-scale private capital. Without this magnetic pull, grant-funded AT ecosystems with high levels of concessional capital can create barriers rather than pathways for breakthrough technologies. We can learn from other sectors such as telecoms, renewable energy, agriculture, and healthcare, where significant private investment enabled agile startups in nascent markets to leapfrog the often bureaucratic, inefficient, and under-resourced public management.

In response, GDI Hub has designed and mobilized an ambitious and sophisticated investment vehicle that provides a viable entry point for commercial investors to explore the AT sector, with above-market returns and downside protection. The AT Growth Fund will invest $100 million into the most promising early to-growth stage AT businesses in LMICs, combined with unparalleled venture support facilities, leading-edge technical and domain expertise, mentorship, coaching, and linkages with regional and global networks for market access. The AT Growth Fund will launch in 2025.

CHAPTER 9

Surpassing the Tipping Point

It takes as much time and energy to dream small as it does to dream big, so you might as well dream big.
—Rosabeth Moss Kanter, sociologist and professor of business at Harvard Business School

As *Case Studies in Disability-Driven Innovation* has demonstrated, the market for disability-centric products and services is global and worth multiple trillions of dollars. Further, the market opportunity is vast, with nearly 2 billion people identifying as disabled and many more having a disability but not disclosing it.

Despite those impressive numbers, the disability market pales in comparison to the global economy. Whereas the buying power of persons with disabilities is roughly $18 trillion, the size of the global economy is more than $100 trillion. The world's population is about 8 billion – four times the number of people identifying as disabled.

Given those facts, the most transformative way to scale disability-driven innovation is to make accessibility and universal design integral to every product and service produced across the economy. Everyone benefits from that all-encompassing innovation.

That is not an argument for lessening the innovation of disability-specific products and services. There are obvious and ongoing needs for disability-driven innovation specific to persons with disabilities, and there is clearly a lucrative market for those products and services.

I also do not want to assert that every entrepreneur or innovator is responsible for taking their venture or their idea to the global marketplace, far from it. They can take their innovation as far as they want to. Writing from personal experience, I have long had my consultancy, Ludke Consulting, LLC. I never once desired Ludke Consulting, LLC to be anything more than a one-person firm offering boutique services to a select number of clients. That is my choice, and I have never regretted it.

However, the hope is that *Case Studies in Disability-Driven Innovation* opens the possibilities and opportunities to those who want to make their idea or their venture into something that has a large-scale impact on markets. The challenge of scaling disability-driven innovation is different from the desire or willpower of entrepreneurs. Instead, the challenge is the myriad of structural barriers that inhibit innovation. Tearing down those barriers is far beyond the means of any one business owner or innovator chasing a dream.

Yet, despite all the obstacles cited in this book (and many more that were not), the reality is that we are very close to reaching the tipping point for mainstreaming disability-driven innovation.

Understanding Tipping Points

In his famous and aptly titled book, *The Tipping Point*, Malcolm Gladwell defined a tipping point as "... the moment of critical mass, the threshold, the boiling point." It is when a seemingly isolated virus explodes into a global pandemic. Or, as Gladwell analogizes, the transformation of the cell phone from a device a few people had in the early 1990s to the economic and cultural phenomenon of the iPhone two decades later.[209]

In the context of disability-driven innovation, a tipping point is that future moment when accessibility and universal design are integrated into every product design and service offering. When competitive, integrated employment becomes the ordinary course of business for organizations of all kinds rather than just a slogan implying an inclusive culture.

Epidemics, societal trends, geo-political conflict, human migration, fashion trends, and ideas all have tipping points.

Reaching a tipping point can happen over years or even seconds. What causes the inflection of many tipping points is a collection of people who bring together different skills and experiences to catalyze change. A tipping point requires a diverse network of actors united around an idea or cause that is more significant than each of them.

The tipping point that started World War I was the instant Archduke Ferdinand of Austria was assassinated in 1914. That was the split second when the simmering diplomatic tensions among the European powers accelerated into armed conflict. The tipping point for curb cuts was when more and more people in places like Berkeley, California, and Denver, Colorado, realized that they, too, benefitted from the actions of activists trying to make their community more accessible. Reaching that tipping point took decades.

Before Malcolm Gladwell's *The Tipping Point*, the most influential study of how the culture of organizations can create tipping points was Rosabeth Moss Kanter's *Men and Women of the Corporation*. Moss Kanter embedded herself into a large, multinational corporation termed "Indsco" (she did not reveal its actual name) in the mid-1970s. While studying the challenges of female employees trying to achieve their version of competitive, integrated employment in Indsco, Moss Kanter found that women isolated within parts of the company had no chance of creating a more inclusive company that no longer discriminated against and tokenized women.

However, she found that departments where just two women worked together could break down internal barriers and stereotypes. Two is the most basic number of people needed to bring about change. Even though two is a shockingly small number, Moss Kanter discovered that two people can collaborate, share experiences and frustrations, and learn from each other. That collaboration could then spawn allyship and broaden a network of like-minded people. Yet, rather than encouraging collaboration, isolating people who were deemed "different" from white males was the norm in Indsco (and almost every 1970s-era conglomerate). "Many organizations currently disperse the available women and spread them over every possible group, as though they are a scarce resource of which each office or group should have at least one", observed Moss Kanter. "However, the policy may be counterproductive for the organizations as well as potentially damaging to the person who is thus forced into the position of token."

In an October 2024 podcast interview, Gladwell upped the number of collaborators needed to crystallize change to three to four people. A crucial part of his rationale for strength and diversity in numbers is it allows people to be themselves. Or, using a concept from earlier in this book, even a small group of collaborators creates psychological safety, which, in turn, drives innovation.[210]

The value proposition Moss Kanter found for gender equality in the 1970s is the same for competitive, integrated employment today, "Organizations with a better balance of people would be more tolerant of the differences among them ... there would be other benefits: a reduction in stress on the people who are 'different,' a reduction in conformity pressures on the dominant groups. It would be more possible, in such an organization, to build the skill and utilize the competence of people who operate at a disadvantage, and thus to vastly enhance the value of an organization's prime resource: its people."[211]

The intriguing aspect in all of this is that when the number of people identifying as disabled is put into the context of the global population, we are very close to a tipping point for disability-driven innovation. Consider how disability can be measured in the context of a population:

- People to identify as disabled
- People to identify as disabled, plus friends and family
- People who identify as disabled, plus those who are disabled but do not disclose a disability
- Everyone is disabled regardless of self-identification, plus friends and family

In any of those three scenarios, persons with disabilities are anywhere from 20 percent to at least 40 percent of the world's population – which is around the numbers Moss Kanter and Gladwell cite as critical mass for triggering change.

Now it is time to explore ways disability-driven innovation reaches its tipping point to the benefit of all people.

5 Steps to Surpass the Tipping Point of Disability-Driven Innovation

This journey concludes with five steps to reach and ultimately exceed the tipping point of disability-driven innovation. When that tipping point is breached, disability-driven innovation will be integrated into all facets of the economy. It will become integral to how we live, work, collaborate, and engage as a society. Accessible and universally designed products will no longer be treated as a niche market and serve only a segment of the population. Further, the essential ingredients to foster disability-driven innovation – such as psychological safety, more equitable access to social and financial capital, less siloed ways of innovating, and open opportunities, to name a few – will be prevalent and available to all.

The five steps outlined in the coming pages are big, systemic ideas. All are challenging to achieve. In many cases, the steps require us to address the fundamentals of how we innovate. They are not tactical. Instead, they involve modernizing organizational strategy and future-proofing our ways of turning ideas into value-generating products and services.

Step #1: Change the Definition of Innovation

Too often, innovation is associated with brilliant ideas. That assumption is wildly misplaced. As serial entrepreneur Tine Thygesen wrote in *Forbes*,

> *Even the entrepreneurial industry (i.e., those whose job it is to cultivate entrepreneurship) is caught up in the concept of the good idea. They talk about idea competitions, idea feedback, and idea generation. All this gives the impression that the idea is the most important element to success. Nothing could be further from the truth.*
>
> *Instead, it's execution that's the core of entrepreneurship, whether it's done by startups or corporates. Successful entrepreneurs and innovators don't have better ideas than anyone else, but they pursue them more vigorously and actively.*[212]

Disability-driven innovation is no different. The world is not lacking in good ideas to create a more inclusive and accessible society. What needs to be improved is the infrastructure that turns those ideas into reality and does so in a way that simultaneously meets a human need while rewarding the entrepreneur. If you want to be a valued partner to an entrepreneur in the disability space, facilitating a brainstorming session has limited value. Instead, helping the innovator take the following steps from the brainstorming session by providing social and financial capital, mentoring, and growing a network of collaborators is far more impactful and lasting.

As *Case Studies in Disability-Driven Innovation* has shown, innovation comes in many forms. The first case study in this book was about a young adult innovating a way to make his school more accessible. It was about using technology to allow one's artistic talents to thrive despite the ravages of a progressive, fatal disease like ALS. It was about the willingness of a successful entrepreneur to share the lessons learned on her journey so that others can have a similar opportunity. Those innovations create value in everyone's lives, not just a few who happen to strike it rich with one good idea.

Please take a few minutes to reflect on the definition of disability-driven innovation in the Introduction. This definition reflects the input of many people advancing the cause of disability-driven innovation. Hopefully, it will serve as our North Star going forward.

Disability-driven innovation is:

> *A disability-centric process grounded in the principles of inclusive design that is proactively generating new and novel ideas, products, or services that solve a human need, especially for persons with disabilities. It can occur within an organization – intrapreneurial – or outside an organization – entrepreneurial. The innovation may ultimately have a broader market appeal and benefit end users of all kinds. Yet, the initial intent of the innovation starts with meeting an immediate need within the population of people who identify as disabled.*

Step #2: Change the Culture of Innovation

To change the definition of innovation, we must also change the culture around the concept of innovation. The first step in changing the culture around innovation is to get out of the "build a better mousetrap" theory.

Too often, we rush to innovate, and, as a result, we end up playing the Finite Game instead of the Infinite Game. The brands that transcend their industries through innovation and long-term value creation are ones such as Patagonia, Walmart, Mattel, Adobe, Apple, Nvidia, and Microsoft.

Brands that are enduring market leaders "... don't compete in the value-proposition race, trying to lead the category as it's currently defined; they play a different game. Better-mousetraps innovation is guided by quantitative ambitions: Outdo your competitors on existing notions of value. Cultural innovation operates according to qualitative ambitions: Change the understanding of what is considered valuable."[213]

Disability-driven innovation is changing the understanding of what is considered valuable. It is built on concepts like inclusivity, universal design, opportunity, and accessibility. It is not a mystery why so many leading companies incorporate disability-driven innovation into their business model.

Disability-driven innovation also involves creating long-term value. Long-term value creation is not excessive wealth generation for a select few. It is about enriching the socio-economic lives of all people for future generations. It is the difference between running a company like Enron and inventing the typewriter. Enron went bankrupt (in a wildly spectacular fashion) once it became clear the company was built on nothing but fictitious trades in inflated energy markets.

In contrast to the 16-year shell game of Enron, the typewriter has endured for over 200 years. It has done so because the typewriter is an innovation that has enriched countless lives (think of all the letters, poems, news dispatchers, and books written via a typewriter), and it positively impacted how we work and drive economic growth. Plus, its fundamental component – the keyboard – is still with us today and adding value to our lives.

Leaders of organizations who want to improve their culture to spur disability-driven innovation must be particularly sensitive to the perspective of persons with disabilities. Building trust into an innovative culture starts at the top of an organization. The expectations of persons with disabilities for that leadership are very high and rightfully so. Trust is earned, not given.

Step #3: Reorient Our Mindset and Be Accountable for Doing So

A free-market economy has proven time and time again to be the only economic system that endures. However, a market-based economy has significant and widespread flaws. These include excessive wealth creation in the hands of a few, a prioritization of short-term profit over long-term value, and excessive resource consumption to meet immediate consumer demands.

In many ways, the flaws of a free-market economy do not stem from the model itself. The flaws come about due to our application of the model. Our insatiable desire to value the immediate over the future is the root cause of many shortcomings and inequities in our economic systems. Markets do not create leaders focused on the immediacy of the finite game. By themselves, markets do not create gas-guzzling SUVs at the expense of fuel-efficient models. Nor do markets push forward taxpayer-funded bailouts to inept corporations while we fail to invest adequate resources in early childhood education.

Markets are agnostic. They are merely tools we create to engage in innovation and commerce. Rather than blaming markets for our problems, we need an honest dose of reality: Humans create those outcomes by rewarding their underlying behaviors operating within markets.

What we must do is quickly and decisively shift our mindset to one of infinite leadership. Infinite leadership involves innovating for the greater good and using innovation to drive broad-based value creation for everyone, not just a few in privileged positions.

Returning to Simon Sinek's *The Infinite Game*, the costs of prioritizing the finite over the infinite are steep. Transformative innovation for the benefit of many does not happen when we play the finite game. As Sinek powerfully wrote:

> *Because the finite-minded leaders place an unbalanced focus on near-term results, they often employ any strategy or tactic that will help them make the numbers. Some favorite options include reducing investment in research and development, extreme cost-cutting (e.g., regular rounds of layoffs, opting for cheaper, lower quality ingredients in products, cutting corners in manufacturing or quality control), and growth through acquisition and stock buybacks. These decisions, in turn, can shake a company's culture. People start to realize nothing and no one is safe. In response, some instinctually behave as if they were switched to self-preservation mode. They hoard information, hide mistakes, and operate in a more cautious, risk-averse way. To protect themselves, they trust no one...the sum of all these behaviors contributes to a general decline in cooperation across the company, which also leads to a stagnation of any truly new or innovative ideas.*[214]

Self-preservation, winner-take-all, and hoarding information are the exact opposite traits needed to reach the goal of Timothy Clark's challenger safety that was outlined in Chapter 4. Returning to Clark's definition of challenger safety is a helpful reminder of what we must aspire to. Challenger safety "gives you the chance to speak truth to power when you think something needs to change and it's time to say so. Armed with challenger safety, individuals overcome the pressure to conform and can enlist themselves in the creative process." Most significantly, "Challenger safety is the license to innovate."[215]

To its credit, disability-driven innovation is underpinned by a selfless desire to solve human-centric problems. The mindset of the infinite game is very much aligned with this mindset. As Ashton Rosin pointed out in Chapter 1, many founders in recent years have been motivated by a desire to strike it rich with a unicorn-like idea. Probably for good reason, many of those founders were not successful. In contrast, the mindset of ventures in the disability space is focused on fixing problems facing people in an inaccessible society.

Yet, to succeed in transforming the economy and society, disability-driven innovation is entirely reliant on the markets that have shown a timeless tendency to reward those who prioritize the finite over the infinite. Thus, every one of us must hold ourselves and others accountable to avoid the actions that lead to short-termism and finite leadership in driving and scaling innovation.

Step #4: Build Social Capital Through More Effective Networks

If you read Malcolm Gladwell's *Tipping Point* and its successor, *Revenge of the Tipping Point*, about how ideas take hold and spread in society, you come to appreciate that money is not the dominant driver of transformation. Its driver is networks of people who take an interest in the idea, support it, use their personal and professional reputation to advance it, and push others to adopt it.

Consider how we have explored how ideas are generated and spread. Take, for example, the weekend-long hackathon Sandy Lacey and others created to advance human-centered design innovation. Lacey and her collaborators only used a paltry sum of money ($2,500) as a reward to add some fun to the competition. The cost of food and space for the event was nominal, many people traveled on their own dime to attend, and the underlying premise was the ideas had to be bootstrapped with minimal resources.

What made the hackathon so powerful was the people and organizations that participated in it. They brought together a combustible mix of brainpower, different lived experiences, and a passion to innovate solutions. Money had nothing to do with driving the innovative spirit of the hackathon participants.

Yes, money is critical. Just ask Michael Zalle how it felt to take thousands of dollars from his retirement savings to meet YellowBird's payroll. But money is not what powers the widespread adoption of an innovation.

Our connections across our networks are the main ingredient of how transformative innovations enter and shape trillion-dollar global markets and reach billions of customers.

As Malcolm Gladwell has described, the spread of ideas comes from distinct, yet connected, people in networks. Within the networks people have different roles, each one equally important. The "Mavens" are the experts, the "Connectors" are the ones who bring people and organizations of all backgrounds together, and the "Salespersons" are the ones able to translate the idea or the innovation into a compelling narrative that makes others want to get behind it. Those relationships are central to the social capital needed for an innovative idea to reach the tipping point of market disruption.

Persons with disabilities are powerful innovators – often borne out of necessity. But the challenge for many is they do not have the diverse and influential networks to mainstream an idea or an innovation. Hopefully, each of you reading this book can become part of those networks and help them flourish.

Step #5: Bring Grace and Humility to the Journey of Innovation

We all need to bring more grace and humility to the innovation journey. The psychological safety necessary for innovation demands it. We must be comfortable with being challenged, people inadvertently speaking in a way that may not be entirely respectful of disability, and people not understanding the nuance of disability. However, getting past those concerns is necessary if the disability community is to broaden its networks and grow the social capital needed to scale disability-driven innovation.

Joseph Jones, Chief of Staff, President's Office, Des Moines University, shared a compelling insight in our conversation while writing *Case Studies in Disability-Driven Innovation*. His words are ones we can all aspire to live by in our journey of innovation,

> *We're going to be interacting with the business leaders and others who want to do more. They believe in disability rights. They want innovation to succeed. And they are here to learn. They don't have the experiences we've had. They don't understand some of the nuances we do. They don't understand the communication of disability. As a result, they will say some things that we think are inappropriate. They will present some things as the gold standard for what they've done to pat themselves on the back.*

> *But we must remember we are not here to throw back discrimination at them or look down on them. What we're going to do is meet them where they are. We're going to model good behavior. We're going to model the types of language we want to be used. But if we start throwing back at them and say, 'You're doing this, this, and this wrong.' they will not feel included in this movement. What we want*

is for them to be comfortable putting their toe in the water. And then put more of their toes in the water. Then a whole foot and then a leg into the water, so they can realize that it's okay. The water's fine. We want them to say to us, "I want to find ways to work with you to make all our lives better."

Eric Ingram and the Limitless Potential of Disability-Driven Innovation

This case study is intentionally the last one in *Case Studies in Disability-Driven Innovation*. It is a lesson in optimism, showing how the life experiences of people with disabilities form unique and powerful talents. It also takes us to the cutting edge of space-based technology. Eric Ingram's story also brings us full circle in the book. Just like the stories of Archer Archer, Michale Zalle, and Erica Cole in the Introduction, Eric Ingram used his disability as a superpower to achieve something truly innovative that would benefit many.

Ingram is a trailblazing entrepreneur and advocate for accessibility in space exploration. As the Founder of Scout Space, he pioneered innovations in orbital safety and cutting-edge technologies to enhance space domain awareness. Scout originated to meet a very unique need – to de-risk orbital flight. "Space is very crowded these days," said Ingram. "There are a lot of satellites, debris, and junk floating around. So, we help provide situational awareness while in space."

Scout has two product lines. First, are its short-range products that allow spacecraft – or the people that own and operate them – to see and understand things around them while in orbit. Ingram refers to this as "Local Situational Awareness". The second product line goes on larger satellites and tracks other objects (such as satellites owned and operated by national security agencies of other countries) for intelligence-gathering purposes. This is called "Space Domain Awareness". As

Ingram helpfully noted, one way to differentiate the products is to treat the short-range products like smart dashcams in your car, while the long-range products like traffic cameras at intersections.

Launched in early 2019, Ingram and the Scout team faced the unenviable twin challenge of not only starting a business but doing so just as COVID-19 spread worldwide. "When I founded Scout I was still at the Federal Aviation Administration, so it was a side business for me," recalled Ingram. "But in late 2019, I quit my job to focus full-time on Scout. And then a few months later the world shut down. We were in survival mode. For that first year, we did all the usual things that many entrepreneurs do...I raided my savings to float the company, and we basically volunteered our time."

Impressively, Scout's dark days were short-lived. By 2021, Scout was on a path to sustained success. Eric and the Scout team were accepted into the TechStars accelerator community – on their third try – in 2021. Scout also landed its first government contract that year and sent its first payload into space – a payload constructed in the living room of the then-COO's house and by a virtual team ordering parts online.

"I would not say my disability gave me any special technical skills to do my job better or to create a better version of Scout," said Ingram. "But what my disability gave me was the life experiences, disposition, and creativity to constantly deal with all the hurdles that come with starting a business. My disability aided my mindset. It allowed me to go from a disappointing meeting with one investor to the next meeting where I had to find the willpower to put a smile on my face and lead with energy. Even before I started my career I knew how to celebrate the wins and quickly move on from the losses."

After six years of leadership at Scout, including five as CEO and a year as Chief Strategy Officer, in January 2025, Ingram successfully transitioned the company into the hands of a capable leadership team, achieving the rare milestone of creating a self-sustaining enterprise.

Ingram's passion for innovation and improving society will not soon lessen. He is also a leader in AstroAccess, working to make space accessible for all, especially disabled individuals. Beyond aerospace, Ingram has served as President of the U.S. Wheelchair Rugby Association, demonstrating his commitment to leadership in both sports and advocacy. His life's mission is to break barriers – earthly and celestial.[216]

Final Thoughts: Scaling Disability-Driven Innovation Falls on All of Us

Despite the ambitious nature of these five steps, all of us can – and must – play a role in making them a reality. As Malcolm Gladwell noted in *The Tipping Point*, no single event occurred by itself. Nor has there ever been a single person who transformed society. Not everyone is an innovator like Thomas Edison or Temple Grandin. CEOs like Steve Jobs are the rarest of the rare. Very few people could unite people and mobilize a movement like Judy Heumann did. Gertrude Ederly's adventurous spirit is not found in many people. But all of us – together – can create and scale our networks so that our combined skills and lived experiences can transform the world for the better. We can each foster our own curb-cut effect and be the one that helps accelerate the movement to a more accessible and inclusive society – today and far into the future.

Diego Mariscal, the Founder, CEO, and Chief Disabled Officer of 2Gether-International – one of the world's leading startup accelerators for disabled founders – has the honor of concluding *Case Studies in Disability-Driven Innovation*. His powerful story and insightful thoughts beautifully summarize the book.

When I was young, I asked a classmate if he wanted to play with me. He said his dad didn't let him play with "weird" kids. The funny thing is, I don't remember this happening – my mom told me the story years later. I never saw my disability as weird or different; it's always been a natural part of my life. What I do remember, though, is feeling misunderstood and frustrated by how people viewed and treated me differently.

That frustration led me to create my first company, Limitless, to educate others about disability. At the time, I didn't even see myself as an entrepreneur. My dad was an entrepreneur, and I was determined to do anything but follow that path. However, the more I connected with disabled leaders and learned about the disability rights and pride movements, the more I realized something powerful: disability and entrepreneurship are two sides of the same coin. Both require resilience, innovation, and navigating a world not built to fit you.

As disabled people, we have to innovate to survive. From the moment we wake up, we're problem-solving: figuring out how to get dressed, how to communicate, and how to navigate a world that doesn't always accommodate our needs. That kind of tenacity and creativity is also at the heart of entrepreneurship.

What's striking is how many successful entrepreneurs – people like Richard Branson, Elon Musk, and investors on Shark Tank – attribute their success to traits shaped by their disabilities. But this recognition often comes after they've achieved fame and wealth. Imagine a world where we didn't wait until after success to see disability as an asset. Imagine if we recognized and fostered it as a competitive advantage from the start. How many more innovations in education, policy, and accessibility could we unleash?

My friend Judy Heumann always said, "Disability is a natural part of the human experience." Everyone will acquire a disability at some point in their life, and as life expectancy grows, this truth becomes even more universal. Disability brings a unique perspective that can help us tackle some of the world's biggest challenges, like the mental health crisis and climate change. When we lean into the principles of disability – resilience, adaptability, and creativity – we create solutions that benefit not just the disability community but everyone.

Entrepreneurship saved my life. After being kicked out of school and rejected in countless job interviews, I leaned into my skills as a disabled person: persistence, active listening, and a refusal to give up. Growing up, I couldn't walk or run like other kids, so I developed different skills to connect with people. I became a careful, attentive listener because I had to rely on conversation to engage with the world in ways others didn't. That heightened ability to listen and communicate became a strength I carry with me today, shaping how I lead and build relationships. It wasn't until I embraced my disability as a competitive advantage that 2Gether-International began to thrive.

The stories in this book illustrate that disability isn't just a challenge; it's a wellspring of innovation and creativity. We're all one accident or life experience away from discovering its power. My hope is that we can unlock and unleash that potential together.

Notes

[1] Case study is based on a September 3, 2024 interview with Archer Archer and material on www.ArcherArcher.org.

[2] Greenberg, R. (2024, October 8). *5 Surefire Ways to Fail at Entrepreneurship (Even with a Great Idea or Product)*. Medium. https://ehandbook.com/5-surefire-ways-to-fail-at-entrepreneurship-even-with-a-great-idea-or-product-f5b1d533ffe5

[3] Phills, J. et al. (2008, Fall) Rediscovering Social Innovation. Stanford Social Innovation Review. https://ssir.org/articles/entry/rediscovering_social_innovation

[4] Ibid.

[5] Rogers, E. (1995*). Diffusion of Innovations*. (Fifth Edition). Free Press. p. 12.

[6] Ibid. p. 37.

[7] Jeetah, R. (2022) Making the Case for Disability Innovation: Opportunity at Concrete Change for the Disabled Community. *Open Journal of Social Sciences*, 10, 111-125. doi: 10.4236/jss.2022.102007.

[8] (2024, June 9). Disability innovation challenges Inclusive Design: Unlocking Entrepreneurial Opportunities in Disability Innovation. Fastercapital.com. https://fastercapital.com/content/Disability-innovation-challenges-Inclusive-Design--Unlocking-Entrepreneurial-Opportunities-in-Disability-Innovation.html#Understanding-Disability-Innovation-Challenges

[9] Fry, H. (host). (2023, March 22). The Future with Hannah Fry, *Bloomberg*, https://www.bloomberg.com/news/videos/2023-03-23/technology-and-ai-for-social-inclusion-the-future-with-hannah-fry-episode-5-digital?sref=RUHCvAuz

[10] Interview with Keely Cat-Wells, November 5, 2024.

[11] Glette, M. K., & Wiig, S. (2022). The Headaches of Case Study Research: A Discussion of Emerging Challenges and Possible Ways Out of the Pain. The Qualitative Report, 27(5), 1377-1392. https://doi.org/10.46743/2160-3715/2022.5246

[12] Girma, H. (2017, September 13). Break down disability barriers to spur growth and innovation. *Financial Times*. https://www.ft.com/content/d8997604-97ab-11e7-8c5c-c8d8fa6961bb

[13] Interview with Eric Ingram, January 7, 2025.

[14] Adapted from "Emilea, a vibrant young woman with an infectious personality, is the owner of Em's Coffee Co.". Griffinhammis.com. https://www.griffinhammis.com/self-employment-ems-coffee-company/

[15] Ibid.

[16] Interview with Em Hillman and Tami Fenner, October 16, 2024.

[17] Interview with Regina Kline, September 27, 2023.

[18] Interview with Ashlea Lantz, November 6, 2023.

[19] Larsson, M. (2023). *How Building the Future Really Works*: Self-Published.

[20] Howe Innovation Center (2023). Defining DisabilityTech: The Rise of Inclusive Innovation. p. 7. https://www.perkins.org/disabilitytech-making-the-world-more-accessible-for-everyone/

[21] Interview with Chris Maher, October 3, 2024.

[22] Excerpt From: Jessica Elisabeth Murphy. "Disability at a Glance 2023." Apple Books. p. 47.

[23] Sherbin, L. and Kennedy, J. (2017). "Disabilities and Inclusion". Center for Talent Innovation (now Coqual). https://www.coqual.org/wp-content/uploads/2020/09/CoqualDisabilitiesInclusion_KeyFindings090720.pdf

[24] Alemany, L. and Vermeulen, F. (July - August 2023). "Disability as a Source of Competitive Advantage." *Harvard Business Review*. https://hbr.org/2023/07/disability-as-a-source-of-competitive-advantage

[25] Return on Disability (2024, September 20). Global Economics of Disability Report: 2024. p. 8 https://www.rod-group.com/wp-content/uploads/2024/09/The-Global-Economics-of-Disability-2024-The-Return-on-Disability-Group-September-24-2024.pdf?https%3A%2F%2Fwww.rod-group.com%2Fresearch-insights%2Fannual-report-2024%2F

[26] Vantage Market Research (October 2023). "Assistive Technology Market – Global Industry Assessment & Forecast." https://www.vantagemarketresearch.com/industry-report/assistive-technology-market-1786#:~:text=Market%20Synopsis,USD%2031.22%20Billion%20by%202030.

[27] Accenture (October 2018). "Getting to Equal 2018: The Disability Inclusion Advantage". https://www.accenture.com/content/dam/accenture/final/a-com-migration/pdf/pdf-89/accenture-disability-inclusion-research-report.pdf

[28] Global Economics of Disability Report: 2024. p. 20.

[29] Walmart (2018). "Your Story is Our Story. Culture Diversity & Inclusion 2018 Report". https://corporate.walmart.com/content/dam/corporate/documents/purpose/culture-diversity-equity-and-inclusion-report/walmart-cdi-report-vfweb.pdf

[30] Malloy Deaderick, D. (2023, November 7). Small Changes, Big Impact: Sensory-Friendly Hours Return. Walmart.com. https://corporate.walmart.com/news/2023/11/07/small-changes-big-impact-sensory-friendly-hours-return

[31] Interview with Victor Calise on September 24, 2024.

[32] Walmart. (2024, September 12). Walmart Raises the Bar for Inclusive Shopping with Specialized Caroline's Carts in Missouri [Press Release]. https://www.businesswire.com/news/home/20240912723861/en/Walmart-Raises-the-Bar-for-Inclusive-Shopping-with-Specialized-Carolines-Carts-in-Missouri

[33] Aira (n.d.). Aira Pilot Launches at All Locations in California, Texas, and Florida! Aira.io. https://aira.io/aira-at-walmart/

[34] Interview with Robin Tim Weis, October 19, 2024.

[35] Barbie Fast Facts. Barbiemedia.com. https://www.barbiemedia.com/about-barbie/fast-facts.html

[36] Janjuha-Jivraj, S. (2023, July 24). How Mattel Reinvented Barbie to Become A Global Icon. Forbes. https://www.forbes.com/sites/shaheenajanjuhajivrajeurope/2023/07/24/how-mattel-reinvented-barbie-to-become-a-global-icon/

[37] Ibid.

[38] Rodriguez-Vila, O., Nickerson, D., & Bharadwaj, S. (May – June 2024). How Inclusive Brands Fuel Growth. Harvard Business Review. https://hbr.org/2024/05/how-inclusive-brands-fuel-growth

[39] Interview with Michelle Sagan, September 16, 2024.

[40] Interview with Kayla McKeon, October 29, 2024.

[41] Davis Smith, J. (2023, April 7). *A Barbie with Down syndrome is already selling out. Here's how kids with the genetic disorder are reacting.* Yahoo.com. https://www.yahoo.com/lifestyle/barbie-down-syndrome-already-selling-220238515.html

[42] Eislund, S. and Caballero, N. (2022) Curb Cuts: A Brief History. *Accessibility Digest.* Spring 2022. Issue 2. https://www.carleton.edu/accessibility-resources/newsletter/curb-cuts-a-brief-history/

[43] Mars, R. (Host). (2021, April 27). Curb Cuts (No. 308) 99% Invisible. https://99percentinvisible.org/episode/curb-cuts/

[44] Blackwell, A. (2017). The Curb Cut Effect. Stanford Social Innovation Review. Winter 2017. https://ssir.org/articles/entry/the_curb_cut_effect#bio-footer

[45] Mars, R. Curb Cuts.

[46] All You Need to Know About ADA Curb Ramp Requirements in 2021. ADASolutions.com. https://adatile.com/all-you-need-to-know-about-ada-curb-ramp-requirements/

[47] Ibid.

[48] Rani, M. (2024, July 11). Steve Gleason breaks creative boundaries for the ALS community with Adobe Firefly. Adobe Blog: Customer Stories. https://blog.adobe.com/en/publish/2024/07/11/steve-gleason-breaks-creative-boundaries-als-community-with-adobe-firefly

[49] Shi. J. (2023, March 7). Shanghai lawmakers listen to foreign firms on accessible facilities. *ChinaDaily.com.* https://global.chinadaily.com.cn/a/202303/07/WS640691e9a31057c47ebb2b40.html

[50] Dunne, B. (2021, May 5). "Disabled People Question Nike Over FlyEase Shoes. Complex.com. https://www.complex.com/sneakers/a/brendan-dunne/nike-go-flyease-sneakers-for-disabled-people

[51] Satell, G. (2024, March 16). Change Can Come from Anywhere. Medium.com. https://greg-satell.medium.com/change-can-come-from-anywhere-055c1f2033f9

[52] Satell, G. (2019, July 14). True Transformation Isn't Top Down or Bottom Up, But Side-to-Side. DigitalTono.com. https://digitaltonto.com/2019/true-transformation-isnt-top-down-or-bottom-up-but-side-to-side/

[53] Bakshy, Eytan. et. al. (2011, February 9). Everyone's an Influencer: Quantifying Influence on Twitter. *ACM Digital Library*. https://dl.acm.org/doi/10.1145/1935826.1935845

[54] Beichert, M. et. al. (2024, August 22, 2024). The Surprising ROI of Small Online Influencers. MIT Sloan Management Review. https://sloanreview.mit.edu/article/the-surprising-roi-of-small-online-influencers/#:~:text=We%20found%20that%20despite%20their,average%20%E2%80%94%20an%20ROI%20of%20six.

[55] Interview with Giorgi Dzneladze, October 16, 2024.

[56] The Arc, https://thearc.org/about-us/press-center/

[57] Americans with Disabilities Act of 1990 (Original Text), U.S. Equal Employment Opportunity Commission, https://www.eeoc.gov/americans-disabilities-act-1990-original-text

[58] "What does 'regarded as' having a disability mean?", ADA National Network, https://adata.org/faq/what-does-regarded-having-disability-mean

[59] Disabilities: Definition, Types and Models of Disability, Disabled World, https://www.disabled-world.com/disability/types/

[60] Traumatic Brain Injury, National Institute of Neurological Disorders and Stroke, https://www.ninds.nih.gov/health-information/disorders/traumatic-brain-injury-tbi

[61] Ladau, E. (2021). *Demystifying Disability* (p.19). Ten Speed Press.

[62] Interview with Allison Aslan, Disability Program Analyst, Office of Global Programs, U.S. Department of State, September 7, 2024.

[63] Yusuf, Dikko, "Why Multiply Marginalized People with Disabilities Should be Prioritized Before, During and After Disasters and Emergencies," wid.org, https://wid.org/why-multiply-marginalized-people-with-disabilities-should-be-prioritized-before-during-and-after-disasters-and-emergencies/

[64] Stein, P.J.S., Stein, M.A., Groce, N. *et al.* The role of the scientific community in strengthening disability-inclusive climate resilience. *Nat. Clim. Chang.* 13, 108–109 (2023). https://doi.org/10.1038/s41558-022-01564-6

[65] "Typewriters and Assistive Technology for Blind and Partially Sighted People," Science Museum, October 28, 2021, https://www.sciencemuseum.org.uk/objects-and-stories/everyday-wonders/typewriters-blind-partially-sighted-people

66 "Informal economy," International Labour Organization, https://www.ilo.org/global/programmes-and-projects/prospects/themes/informal-economy/lang--en/index.htm#:~:text=The%20informal%20economy%20refers%20to,gender%20inequality%20and%20precarious%20work.

67 Gunawan, T., & Rezki, J. (2022). Mapping Workers with Disabilities in Indonesia Policy Suggestions and Recommendations. Www.ilo.org. https://www.ilo.org/sites/default/files/wcmsp5/groups/public/@asia/@ro-bangkok/@ilo-jakarta/documents/publication/wcms_836028.pdf

68 Crespo, Ana, Vidal, Laia and Greedy, Martin (translator) (2021). "Inclusion of persons with disabilities in Latin America and the Caribbean" (p. 26). World Bank Group, p. 26, 2021. https://thedocs.worldbank.org/en/doc/29c1baaa285d50c71ea1efeb259248ff-0370062021/original/Disability-Inclusion-in-Latin-America-and-the-Caribbean-Easy-Read-Version.pdf

69 Robert Neuwirth's *Stealth of Nations: The Global Rise of the Informal Economy* is an excellent resource to better understand the informal economy.

70 Interview with Brian Mwenda, founder and CEO of Hope Tech, October 8, 2024.

71 Ellen MacArthur Foundation (n.d.). How does the circular economy create value? www.ellenmacarthurfoundation.org. https://www.ellenmacarthurfoundation.org/how-does-the-circular-economy-create-value

72 Mace, M. (2021, July 19). Circular economy attracting $1.3trn in annual investments, but dwarfed by linear spending models. www.Edie.net. https://www.edie.net/circular-economy-attracting-1-3trn-in-annual-investments-but-dwarfed-by-linear-spending-models/#:~:text=B%20Corp-,Circular%20economy%20attracting%20$1.3trn%20in%20annual%20investments%2C%20but%20dwarfed,of%20consumption%20and%20resource%20use.

73 Interview with Katherine Toops on September 25, 2024.

74 Interview with Keely Cat-Wells, November 4, 2024.

75 Interview with Joe Quintanilla, September 29, 2023.

76 Material taken from interview with Amanda Myers, October 29, 2024, content provided by the Kansas City Royals, and information from www.kcdsi.org.

77 "Disability and Employment, Fact Sheet 1," United Nations, https://www.un.org/development/desa/disabilities/resources/factsheet-on-persons-with-disabilities/disability-and-employment.html

78 Bureau of Labor Statistics, February 23, 2023, *Persons with a Disability: Labor Force Characteristics – 2022*, [Press Release], https://www.bls.gov/news.release/pdf/disabl.pdf

79 Ibid.

80 Ibid.

81 Ibid., p. 4.

[82] Work Without Limits, UMass Chan Medical School, (2022) Quick Tips: Disclosure vs. Self-Identification, https://workwithoutlimits.org/wp-content/uploads/2022/08/Disclosure-vs-Self-ID-2022.pdf

[83] Interview with James Warnken, September 4, 2024.

[84] Interview with Mike Hess, August 29, 2024.

[85] "Accommodations and Productivity: The case against disclosure". (October 8, 2023). Return on Disability. https://www.rod-group.com/research-insights/accommodations-and-productivity-the-case-against-disclosure/

[86] Clark, T. (2020). The 4 Stages of Psychological Safety (pp. 4-13). Berrett-Koehler Publishing.

[87] Ibid., p. 113.

[88] Alemany, L. and Vermeulen, F. (July - August 2023). "Disability as a Source of Competitive Advantage." Harvard Business Review. https://hbr.org/2023/07/disability-as-a-source-of-competitive-advantage

[89] Interview with Hannah Bouline, Director of Impact and Sustainability, Vertical Harvest, October 9, 2024.

[90] Disabled World, "Models of Disability: Types and Definitions," https://www.disabled-world.com/definitions/disability-models.php

[91] University of Oregon Accessible Education Center, "Medical and Social Models of Disability," https://aec.uoregon.edu/content/medical-and-social-models-disability

[92] Interview with Ashlea Lantz, November 6, 2023.

[93] Dunne, Maureen, "Building the Neurodiversity Talent Pipeline for the Future of Work," *MIT Sloan Management Review*, November 28, 2023, https://sloanreview.mit.edu/article/building-the-neurodiversity-talent-pipeline-for-the-future-of-work/#article-authors. In her article Dunne cited M. Stolte, V. Trindade-Pons, P. Vlaming, et al., "Characterizing Creative Thinking and Creative Achievements in Relation to Symptoms of Attention-Deficit/Hyperactivity Disorder and Autism Spectrum Disorder," Frontiers in Psychiatry 13 (July 1, 2022): 1-15.

[94] Ives-Rublee, Mia, et. al., "Removing Obstacles for Disabled Workers Would Strengthen the U.S. Labor Market," Center for American Progress, May 24, 2022, https://www.americanprogress.org/ article/removing-obstacles-for-disabled-workers-would-strengthen-the-u-s-labor-market/

[95] Interview with Gina Kline, November 9, 2020.

[96] "Getting to Equal: The Disability Inclusion Advantage," Accenture, October 29, 2018, p. 4, https://www.accenture.com/content/dam/accenture/final/a-com-migration/pdf/pdf-89/accenture-disability-inclusion-research-report.pdf

[97] European Parliament (March 2018). Equality and the Fight against Racism and Xenophobia. Think Tank European Parliament. p. 35.

https://www.europarl.europa.eu/RegData/etudes/STUD/2018/615660/EPRS_STU(2018)615660_EN.pdf

[98] United Nations Economic and Social Commission for Asia and the Pacific. (n.d.). *Building Disability-Inclusive Societies in Asia and the Pacific.* unescap.org. p. 1. https://www.unescap.org/sites/default/files/publications/SDD%20BDIS%20report%20A4%20v14-5-E.pdf

[99] Deloitte Access Economics. (August 2011). *The economic benefits of increasing employment for people with disability.* Commissioned by the Australian Network on Disability. https://and.org.au/wp-content/uploads/2021/10/Economic-benefits-of-increasing-employment-for-people-with-disability_Aug11.pdf

[100] The World Bank Group. (December 2, 2021). *Inclusion of Persons with Disabilities is Crucial for the Sustainable Development of Latin America and the Caribbean.* [Press release]. https://www.worldbank.org/en/news/press-release/2021/12/02/la-inclusion-de-las-personas-con-discapacidad-clave-para-el-desarrollo-sostenible-de-america-latina-y-el-caribe

[101] The World Bank Group (n.d.). Breaking Barriers - Disability Inclusion in Latin America and the Caribbean. https://www.worldbank.org/en/region/lac/publication/rompiendo-barreras#:~:text=In%20economic%20terms%20alone%2C%20available,build%20a%20more%20inclusive%20future.

[102] United Nations, "Inequality – Bridging the Divide," https://www.un.org/en/un75/inequality-bridging-divide

[103] Ingraham, Christopher, "How rising inequality hurts everyone, even the rich," *Washington Post*, February 6, 2018, https://www.washingtonpost.com/news/wonk/wp/2018/02/06/how-rising-inequality-hurts-everyone-even-the-rich/

[104] De Smet, Aaron, et. al., "The Great Attrition is making hiring harder. Are you searching the right talent pools?" McKinsey & Company, July 13, 2022, https://www.mckinsey.com/capabilities/people-and-organizational-performance/our-insights/the-great-attrition-is-making-hiring-harder-are-you-searching-the-right-talent-pools

[105] Kaufman, Jonathan, "Mindset Matters: The Future of Work, Disability, And Imagining What's Next," *Forbes*, December 3, 2020.

[106] Lorenzo, Rocío, et. al., "How Diverse Leadership Teams Boost Innovation," Boston Consulting Group, January 23, 2018, https://www.bcg.com/publications/2018/how-diverse-leadership-teams-boost-innovation

[107] Goodman, Nanette, et. al., "The Extra Costs of Living with a Disability in the U.S. – Resetting the Policy Table," National Disability Institute, October 2020, p.1, https://www.nationaldisabilityinstitute.org/wp-content/uploads/2020/10/extra-costs-living-with-disability-brief.pdf

[108] "ADB Briefs No. 204, Disability and Social Protections in Asia," Asian Development Bank, December 2021, p. 3, https://www.adb.org/sites/default/files/publication/760671/adb-brief-203-disability-social-protection-asia.pdf

[109] "Inclusion of persons with disabilities in Latin America and the Caribbean," pp. 29-33.

[110] Stephane, Joanne (Deloitte Consulting, LLP) and Kenji Yoshino (Meltzer Center for Diversity, Inclusion, and Belonging at the New York University School of Law), "Uncovering culture: A call to action for leaders", 2023, pp. 4 – 7, https://www2.deloitte.com/content/dam/Deloitte/us/Documents/about-deloitte/dei/us-uncovering-culture-a-call-to-action-for-leaders.pdf?dl=1

[111] Ibid., p. 10.

[112] Anderson, E. (2015, March 4-5). "Liberty, Equality, and Private Government". Delivered at The Tanner Lectures in Human Values. Princeton University, Princeton, New Jersey, United States.

[113] Deloitte Report p. 13.

[114] Thompson, Vilissa, The Century Foundation, "Testimony before the House Committee on Financial Services, Subcommittee on Diversity and Inclusion, Hearing on Diversity Includes Disability: Exploring Inequities in Financial Services for Persons with Disabilities, Including Those Newly Disabled Due to Long-Term COVID," May 24, 2022, https://tcf.org/content/commentary/removing-economic-barriers-for-disabled-people-requires-understanding-intersectionality/

[115] Vallas, Rebecca, et. al., "Economic Justice Is Disability Justice," The Century Foundation, April 21, 2022, https://tcf.org/content/report/economic-justice-disability-justice/

[116] Schweitzer, Justin, et. al., "How Dehumanizing Administrative Burdens Harm Disabled People," Center for American Progress," December 5, 2022, https://www.americanprogress.org/article/how-dehumanizing-administrative-burdens-harm-disabled-people/

[117] Ibid.

[118] Ibid.

[119] Laurence, Bethany, "Income Limits for SSDI Benefits," disabilitysecrets.com, 2023, https://www.disabilitysecrets.com/resources/social-security-disability/ssdi/income-limits-ssdi-benefits

[120] Romig, Kathleen, et. al., "The Case for Updating SSI Asset Limits," Center on Budget and Policy Priorities, July 25, 2023, https://www.cbpp.org/sites/default/files/6-26-23socsec.pdf

[121] Interview with Sara Hart Weir, October 22, 2024.

[122] "Poverty and Social Exclusion of Persons with Disabilities European Human Rights Report Issue 4 - 2020,", p. 53.

[123] European Commission, Directorate-General for Employment, Social Affairs and Inclusion, Baptista, Isabel, Marlier, Eric, "Social protection for people with disabilities – An analysis

of policies in 35 countries," Publications Office of the European Union, 2022, pp. 11-15, https://data.europa.eu/doi/10.2767/323350

[124] "ADB Briefs No. 204, Disability and Social Protections in Asia," p. 4.

[125] Interview with James Warnken, September 5, 2024.

[126] U.S. Commission on Civil Rights, "Subminimum Wages: Impacts on the Civil Rights of People with

Disabilities," September 2020, pp. 12-16, https://www.usccr.gov/files/2020/2020-09-17-Subminimum-Wages-Report.pdf

[127] Ibid., p. 16.

[128] Morris, A. (2024, August 30). Some disabled workers in the U.S. make pennies per hour. It's legal. *Washington Post.* https://www.washingtonpost.com/wellness/2024/08/30/subminimum-wage-disabled-workers/

[129] Ibid.

[130] Interview with Regina Kline, September 27, 2023.

[131] Shapiro, J. (2024, October 2). This disabled woman built a career. A federal program that helped now penalizes her. npr.org. https://www.npr.org/2024/10/01/g-s1-25453/social-security-ssi-disabilities-work-outdated

[132] Interview with Sara Hart Weir, October 23, 2024.

[133] Touzet, C. (2023, November). "Using AI to support people with disabilities in the labour market: Opportunities and challenges". OECD Artificial Intelligence Papers. No. 7. file:///Users/robertludke/Downloads/008b32b7-en.pdf

[134] Schur LA, Ameri M, Kruse D. Telework After COVID: A "Silver Lining" for Workers with Disabilities? J Occup Rehabil. 2020 Dec;30(4):521-536. doi: 10.1007/s10926-020-09936-5. Epub 2020 Nov 6. PMID: 33156435; PMCID: PMC7645902.

[135] Schwartz, Nelson (2020, September 6). Working From Home Poses Hurdles for Employees of Color. New York Times. https://www.nytimes.com/2020/09/06/business/economy/working-from-home-diversity.html

[136] Ibid.

[137] Aichner, T. The economic argument for hiring people with disabilities. Humanit Soc Sci Commun 8, 22 (2021). https://doi.org/10.1057/s41599-021-00707-y

[138] Interview with Steve Foresti, Senior Advisor, Wilshire Associates, March 30, 2022.

[139] Brooks, D. (2024, September 8). "You Have to Secure The Bag By 50 in this Harsh Corporate Environment." medium.com. https://deanmaxbrooks.medium.com/you-have-to-secure-the-bag-by-50-in-this-harsh-corporate-climate-1e77e21eff82

[140] IBM. (2023, October 12). "Understanding the different types of artificial intelligence". https://www.ibm.com/think/topics/artificial-intelligence-types

[141] Rowan, J. "New decides next: Moving from potential to performance. Deloitte's State of Generative AI in the Enterprise Quarter three report". Deloitte.com, p. 8. https://www2.deloitte.com/content/dam/Deloitte/us/Documents/consulting/us-state-of-gen-ai-q3.pdf https://www2.deloitte.com/content/dam/Deloitte/us/Documents/consulting/us-state-of-gen-ai-q3.pdf

[142] Aquino, S. (2024, August 23). "AI could be a game changer for people with disabilities". *MIT Technology Review*. https://www.technologyreview.com/2024/08/23/1096607/ai-people-with-disabilities-accessibility/

[143] Touzet, "Using AI to support people with disability in the labour market".

[144] Smith, P. and Smith, L. (October 6, 2020), "Artificial intelligence and disability: too much promise, yet too little substance?". *AI and Ethics*. file:///Users/robertludke/Downloads/s43681-020-00004-5.pdf

[145] Centre for Inclusive Design. (2019, May). The Benefit of Designing for Everyone. https://centreforinclusivedesign.org.au/wp-content/uploads/2021/05/inclusive-design-report-digital-160519.pdf

[146] Khosla, V. (2024, September 20). AI: Dystopia or Utopia? Khosla Ventures. https://www.khoslaventures.com/ai-dystopia-or-utopia/

[147] Welker, Y. (2023, November 3). *Generative AI holds great potential for those with disabilities - but it needs policy to shape it*. World Economic Forum. https://www.weforum.org/agenda/2023/11/generative-ai-holds-potential-disabilities/

[148] NeuroNav. (n.d.). How AI Can Help People with Disabilities. NeuroNav.org. https://neuronav.org/self-determination-blog/how-ai-can-help-people-with-disabilities

[149] Interview via text messages with Austin Hanson, October 28, 2024.

[150] Adobe (2023, May 17). Media Alert: Adobe Scales PDF Accessibility with Adobe Sensei AI. Adobe Newsroom. https://news.adobe.com/news/news-details/2023/media-alert-adobe-scales-pdf-accessibility-with-adobe-sensei-ai

[151] Tabrizi, B. (2015, June 23). 75% of Cross-Functional Teams Are Dysfunctional. Harvard Business Review. https://hbr.org/2015/06/75-of-cross-functional-teams-are-dysfunctional?utm_medium=paidsearch&utm_source=google&utm_campaign=domcontent&utm_term=Non-Brand&tpcc=paidsearch.google.dsacontent&gad_source=1&gclid=Cj0KCQjwxsm3BhDrARIsAMtVz6M8oInwKrZUp3b7eYdtK20_szGsFUh-TPDHSNx7p1zDSVOe8owrX4AaAr7yEALw_wcB

[152] Interview with Joseph Jones, October 31, 2024.

[153] Material taken from an interview with Brian Mwenda on October 8, 2024, www.senseshub.vision, and https://zerocon24.zeroproject.org/participations/317400

[154] Bryant, A. (2010, May 29). For the Chief of Saks, It's Culture That Drives Results. *The New York Times*. https://www.nytimes.com/2010/05/30/business/30corner.html

155 Hocking, Shanna, (2021), "Before Saying 'Yes' to a Job, Consider Company Culture, *Harvard Business Review*, https://hbr.org/2021/07/before-saying-yes-to-a-job-consider-company-culture?utm_medium=paidsearch&utm_source=google&utm_campaign=domcontent&utm_term=Non-Brand&tpcc=paidsearch.google.dsacontent&gad_source=1&gclid=Cj0KCQjw-uK0BhC0ARIsANQtgGOE4gLRVuNA0IFFHkVwKwu2iL-oUaY1s0UrQ0RRV73IWTkJgn6NBVIaAjTHEALw_wcB

156 Walker, A. (2023, January 31). "Motivation for Engineering Organisations". medium.com. https://betterprogramming.pub/motivation-for-engineering-organisations-dd96e2fda22a

157 Lee Yohn, Jessica. (February 6, 2021). "Company Culture Is Everyone's Responsibility". Harvard Business Review. https://hbr.org/2021/02/company-culture-is-everyones-responsibility

158 Ward, Jason, "How fathering a son with disabilities helped Microsoft's CEO transform a company," windowcentral.com, March 2, 2022.

159 Ward, Jason, "Microsoft's 'inclusive design' will increase its focus on accessibility in 2022," windowscentral.com, December 8, 2021.

160 Holeček, Aleš. (October 21, 2022). Continuous innovation for more inclusive work: What's new in Microsoft 365 accessibility, July-September 2022 – plus Ignite. Microsoft.com. https://blogs.microsoft.com/accessibility/microsoft-365-accessibility-10-2022/

161 Smith, Brad, "Doubling down on accessibility: Microsoft's next steps to expand accessibility in technology, the workforce, and workplace," blogs.microsoft.com, April 28, 2021.

162 Microsoft Annual Report 2021.

163 Lay-Flurie, Jenny (October 2, 2023). Creating a more disability-inclusive workplace. Microsoft.com. https://blogs.microsoft.com/on-the-issues/2023/10/02/national-disability-employment-awareness-month-divide/

164 Rousmaniere, D. (2015, February 13). What Everyone Should Know About Office Politics. *Harvard Business Review*. https://hbr.org/2015/02/what-everyone-should-know-about-office-politics?utm_medium=paidsearch&utm_source=google&utm_campaign=domcontent&utm_term=Non-Brand&tpcc=paidsearch.google.dsacontent&gad_source=1&gclid=Cj0KCQjw9Km3BhDjARIsAGUb4nz3rHa9U0amwbcp2fKdehcoYe5zWZsNPisqvJysvcWqNm6Vqt2sspMaAgETEALw_wcB

165 Taylor, A. (2024, February 6). Corporate Advocacy in a Time of Social Outrage. *Harvard Business Review*. https://hbr.org/2024/02/corporate-advocacy-in-a-time-of-social-outrage

[166] Herbert Smith Freehills (2023, October 30). The Future of Work 2023: Activism in the workplace. https://www.herbertsmithfreehills.com/insights/reports/future-of-work-report-2023/fow-2023-activism-in-the-workplace

[167] CareSource (n.d.). *We're creating a workplace without limitations.* careers.caresource.com

[168] Material taken from internal CareSource documents and and interview with Patrice L. Harris and Solomon Parker, November 25, 2024.

[169] Berman, M. (28 October 2021) "What is Digital Technology". *Program Insider.* https://programminginsider.com/what-is-digital-technology/

[170] Rogers, E. (1995). Diffusion of Innovations. (Fifth Edition). Free Press. p, 13.

[171] Aquino, S. (2024, May 30). Search For Fire TV, AI And Accessibility, More In Recent New Interview. Forbes.com. https://www.forbes.com/sites/stevenaquino/2024/05/30/amazon-accessibility-boss-peter-korn-talks-new-ai-search-for-fire-tv-ai-and-accessibility-more-in-recent-new-interview/ and Levine, A. (2024, September 30). How to use Fire TV's new AI-enhanced search feature to find your next show or movie. aboutamazon.com. https://www.aboutamazon.com/news/devices/how-to-use-ai-search-on-fire-tv

[172] Interview with Marianne Dijskhoorn, founder of Welkom Accessibility & Events, September 11, 2024, and information from https://geenbeperkingmeer.nl/english-information/

[173] Phills, J. et al. (2008, Fall) Rediscovering Social Innovation. Stanford Social Innovation Review. https://ssir.org/articles/entry/rediscovering_social_innovation

[174] Dwyer, J. (n.d.). *What is innovation: Why almost everyone defines it wrong.* www.Manifold.Group. https://www.manifold.group/post/what-is-innovation

[175] Landry, L. (2020, October 1). *3 Types of Innovation You Should Know.* https://online.hbs.edu/blog/post/3-types-of-innovation-you-should-know?c1=GAW_CM_NW&source=US_CLIMB_PMAX&cr2=content__-__us__-__climb__-__pmax&kw=climb&cr5&cr6&cr7=t&utm_campaign=content__-__us__-__climb__-__pmax&utm_term=climb&gad_source=1&gclid=Cj0KCQjwzby1BhCQARIsAJ_0t5MVM3nHxFBioPYkRr9KPcbE1s2n-HWq1MZlORQbYF7gyJ3DSeWEq7YaAnquEALw_wcB

[176] Salvador, F. and Sting, F. (2022, September 19). How Your Company Can Encourage Innovation from All Employees. Harvard Business Review. https://hbr.org/2022/09/how-your-company-can-encourage-innovation-from-all-employees?utm_medium=paidsearch&utm_source=google&utm_campaign=domcontent&utm_term=Non-Brand&tpcc=paidsearch.google.dsacontent&gad_source=1&gclid=CjwKCAjwoJa2BhBPEiwA0l0ImJPg8-GmcyFqiTKWGbxT3TvKt_E2thzh_pJ9ctdffe_1dWgkJucAJBoCD0AQAvD_BwE

[177] Pisano, G. (2019, January – February). The Hard Truth About Innovative Cultures, Harvard Business Review. https://hbr.org/2019/01/the-hard-truth-about-innovative-cultures

[178] Gass. R. (2011). *What is Transformation?* robertgass.com. http://stproject.org/wp-content/uploads/2012/03/What_is_Transformation.pdf

[179] Zimmerman, N. (ed). (2022, November 11) Guide: Networking and Collaboration, EntreComp360. file:///Users/robertludke/Downloads/entrecompguideno4-EN-networking-collaboration-final-2023.pdf

[180] Satell, G. (2024, August 10). This Is One Reason Why So Much Business Thinking Is Crap. Medium.com. https://greg-satell.medium.com/this-is-one-big-reason-why-so-much-business-thinking-is-crap-743e90028e8d

[181] Rock, D., & Grant, H. (2016, November 4). *Why Diverse Teams Are Smarter.* https://hbr.org/2016/11/why-diverse-teams-are-smarter?utm_medium=paidsearch&utm_source=google&utm_campaign=domcontent_bussoc&utm_term=Non-Brand&tpcc=domcontent_bussoc&gad_source=1&gbraid=0AAAAAD9b3uQSvd3V3q4urb4lzpPhyX7Qu&gclid=CjwKCAjwooq3BhB3EiwAYqYoEutyXw2mAIyiIE9j2SX4kXVLfg8YidULck5K1TATG3RJHnCOoKT20RoC5SEQAvD_BwE

[182] Reid Hoffman as quoted at the Harvard Business School's "Future Of Business 2024: Exploring What's Next for AI, Innovation, and the World of Work". October 16, 2024.

[183] Somerfield, M. (2024, August 29). "The Lean Startup is a Con". Medium.com. https://medium.com/@somerfield.md/the-lean-startup-is-a-con-c626398e077b

[184] Interview with Chanda Hermanson, November 14, 2024.

[185] Information taken from www.zeroproject.org and Interview with Robin Tim Weis, October 19, 2024.

[186] Interview with Sandy Lacey, November 4, 2024.

[187] Manson, M. (2024, July 1). "How to Make Your Own Luck." Medium.com. https://markmanson.medium.com/how-to-make-your-own-luck-912ae6ab717e

[188] Ferguson, N. (2014, June 9). Networks and Hierarchies. The American Interest, 09(6). https://www.the-american-interest.com/2014/06/09/networks-and-hierarchies/?_ga=2.176720748.850216175.1730992314-2115054888.1730992313&utm_campaign=JM-305&utm_content=rk48mvlz&utm_medium=ED&utm_source=mec

[189] Hackathon summary adapted from interview with Sandy Lacey on November 4, 2024 and Shwayder, M. (2024, March 7). Perkins School for the Blind Teams with MIT to Host Hackathon: The Super Bowl of Accessibility. Watertown News. https://www.watertownmanews.com/2024/03/07/perkins-school-for-the-blind-teams-with-mit-to-host-hackathon-the-super-bowl-of-accessibility/

[190] Content taken from interview with Mike Hess on November 18, 2024, interview with Sarah Mark on December 9, 2024, and workforcenavigators.salesforce.com

[191] Ludke, R. (2020). *Transformative Markets* (p. 43), New Degree Press.

[192] Friedman, T. (2008). *Hot, Flat and Crowded* (p. 244) Farrar, Strauss, and Giroux.

[193] Sacks, J. "The Limits of the Free Market". chabad.org.
https://www.chabad.org/parshah/article_cdo/aid/2093280/jewish/The-Limits-of-the-Free-Market.htm

[194] Hoffman, A. (Spring 2018). The Next Phase of Business Sustainability. *Stanford Social Innovation Review*.
https://ssir.org/articles/entry/the_next_phase_of_business_sustainability

[195] Ibid.

[196] Return on Disability (2024, September 20). The Global Economics of Disability Report: 2024.

[197] "World Population by Country 2023," www.worldpopulationreview.com

[198] "GDP, current prices," International Monetary Fund,
https://www.imf.org/external/datamapper/NGDPD@WEO/OEMDC/ADVEC/WEO WORLD

[199] Case study based on material taken from nbcuniversal.com and multiple conversations with Keely Cat-Wells in 2024.

[200] *Transformative Markets*, pp. 16-17.

[201] Lalljee, J. (2021, December 15). Elon Musk is speaking out against government subsidies. Here's a list of the billions of dollars his businesses have received. *Business Insider*.
https://www.businessinsider.com/elon-musk-list-government-subsidies-tesla-billions-spacex-solarcity-2021-12

[202] Lienert, P. et. al. (2020, September 17). The Musk Method: Learn from partners then go it alone. *Reuters*. https://www.reuters.com/article/us-tesla-batteryday-technology-insight/the-musk-method-learn-from-partners-then-go-it-alone-idUSKBN2680K4

[203] Wu, A., et. al. (2023, May 27). The Story Behind Tesla's Success (TSLA). *Investopedia.com*.
https://www.investopedia.com/articles/personal-finance/061915/story-behind-teslas-success.asp

[204] *Tesla 2020 Impact Report*. p. 52. https://www.tesla.com/ns_videos/2020-tesla-impact-report.pdf

[205] Spicer, J. and Gupta, P. (2010, June 10). Carmaker Tesla's stock zooms 40 percent on first day *Reuters*. https://www.reuters.com/article/us-tesla-ipo/carmaker-teslas-stock-zooms-40-percent-on-first-day-idUSTRE65R2B620100629

[206] Cheney, P. (2018, May 1). How I Learned to Love the Prius. *The Globe and Mail*.

[207] Global Disability Innovation Hub. (2021). Disability Innovation Strategy 2021 – 2024. Disabilityinnovation.com. https://cdn.disabilityinnovation.com/uploads/images/GDI-Hub-Strategy_21-24_2021-08-05-090649_jvxq.pdf?v=1628154409

208 AT2030 (n.d.). A Market Landscape and Strategic Approach to Increasing Access to Eyeglasses in Low- and Middle-Income Countries. AT2030.org. https://at2030.org/static/at2030_core/outputs/Product_Narrative-Eyeglasses_final.pdf

209 Gladwell, M. (2002). *The Tipping Point* (p. 16). Hachette Book Group.

210 Ignatius, A. (Host). (2024, October 10). Malcolm Gladwell's New Take on Tipping Points. (Bonus Episode). In HBR IdeaCast. https://hbr.org/podcast/2024/10/malcolm-gladwells-new-take-on-tipping-points

211 Moss Kanter, R. (1993). *Men and Women of the Corporation* (pp. 280-284). Basic Books.

212 Thygesen. T. (2017, January 24). Forget the Myths: Innovation Isn't Created the Way Most People Think, Forbes.com, https://www.forbes.com/sites/tinethygesen/2017/01/24/innovation-isnt-created-the-way-people-think/

213 Holt, D. (2020, September-October). Cultural Innovation. Harvard Business Review. https://hbr.org/2020/09/cultural-innovation

214 Sinek, S. (2019). The Infinite Game (1st ed., p. 28). Portfolio/Penguin.

215 Clark, T. (2020). The 4 Stages of Psychological Safety (pp. 11-12). Berrett-Koehler Publishing.

216 Material taken from interview with Eric Ingram, January 7, 2025, ericingram.net, and scout.space.